The ABCs of Religion

THE ORIGIN AND DEVELOPMENT OF RELIGIOUS THOUGHT AND PRACTICES

Sherrill Gardner Stevens

© 2016

Published in the United States by Nurturing Faith Inc., Macon GA,

www.nurturingfaith.net.

Library of Congress Cataloging-in-Publication Data is available.

ISBN 978-1-938514-88-3

All rights reserved. Printed in the United States of America

Scripture quotations are from New Revised Standard Version Bible, copyright © 1989 National Council of the Churches of Christ in the United States of America. Used by permission. All rights reserved.

Dedicated to

MARGUERITE GODWIN STEVENS
Lifelong soulmate and encourager
Exemplary mother of
Kathie, Timothy and Sheralyn

Author's Introduction

To help readers be prepared to meet ideas they will find in this book, let me introduce myself. I am an anomaly, which means I cannot be easily classified because I do not fit within any common rule. I am a free-thinker who tries to consider carefully what other people think and say, examine issues as thoroughly as I am able, then come to a conclusion about what I believe.

I am a deeply convinced theist. I have not found any concept about human life and the origin of the material universe that has any foundation in rational thought or scientific search that is adequate and believable to me except a profound faith that a Supreme Spiritual Being is the infinite source of all that exists and of the moral values inherent in human life.

But, about many things, I am an agnostic, which means that infinity is so great that mystery about eternal things makes some things unknowable to us during the human pilgrimage of our physical lives. What "eternity beyond this life" will be like, we cannot comprehend. Let me quote an honored teacher of mine who said to his young son, "We do not know what heaven will be like, but Jesus will be there, and that will be heaven, won't it?"

Above all, I am a devoted Christian, a Jesus theologian, and a free-churchman. I believe there is truth in every religion and that there has been misinterpretation and misuse of every religion by some of its practitioners. However, I believe the supreme revelation of God's self, his nature, his character, and his will and ways for mankind were lived out and exemplified in human incarnation by Jesus of Nazareth. I trust him as my Lord.

Contents

Author's Introduction v
Prologue 1
   Some Words about Words and Origins 2
   The Basis of Religious Beliefs 4
Religion among Primitive Peoples 5
Pre-Monotheistic Religions in Asia 7
   Mesopotamia 7
   The Ancient Religions of Canaan 8
   The Religions of India 8
   Jainism and Buddhism 9
   Classical and Modern Hinduism 11
   The Religions of China 11
   Buddhism in China 12
   Shinto, the Religion of Japan 13
   Zoroastrianism in Persia 13
The Rise of Monotheistic and Revealed Religions 17
   Hebrew Religion/Judaism 17
   Christianity 21
   Islam, the Muslim Religion 23
The Influence of Culture on Religion 27
Religious Thought Before Jesus—A Summary 31
The Development of Some Theological Differences 35
   About the Origin of the Material Universe 35
   About the Nature of God 36
   About the Problem of Evil 39
The Development of Sacred Writings in the Hebrew Religion 41
   A Beginning Look at "Sacred" Writings 41
   The Hebrew Scriptures and the Old Testament Canon 43
      Background 43
      Early References to Sacred Hebrew Writings 44
      Organization of the Documents in the Hebrew Scriptures 44

A Brief Description of the Individual Documents............................45
    Genesis 45
    Exodus...45
    Leviticus 46
    Numbers...46
    Deuteronomy 46
    Joshua 46
    Judges 46
    Ruth 47
    I & II Samuel and I & II Kings...47
    I & II Chronicles 47
    Ezra/Nehemiah 47
    Esther 48
    Job..48
    Psalms...49
    Proverbs 49
    Ecclesiastes...49
    Song of Solomon 49
    Isaiah 49
    Jeremiah...50
    Lamentations 50
    Ezekiel 50
    Daniel...50
    Hosea..51
    Joel 51
    Amos 51
    Obadiah..51
    Jonah 51
    Micah 52
    Nahum 52
    Habakkuk 52
    Zephaniah..52
    Haggai 53
    Zechariah...53
    Malachi..53
Observations 53

A Group of Documents Called the Apocrypha 55
The Sweep of History in the Apocrypha 55
The Traditional Documents of the Apocrypha 56

    Tobit "God Is My Good" 56
    Judith 56
    The Rest of Esther 56
    Wisdom of Solomon 56
    Ecclesiasticus/The Wisdom of Sirach 57
    Baruch 57
    Letter of Jeremiah 57
    Greek Additions to Daniel 57
    I Maccabees 58
    II Maccabees 58
    III Maccabees 58
    IV Maccabees 59
    I Esdras 59
    II Esdras 59
    Prayer of Manasseh 59
    Psalm 151 (only seven verses) 59
    Summary 60

Earliest Christian Developments 61
    The Disciples' First Experiences 61
    Fundamental Truths Jesus Left with Them 62
    The Beginning of Church Life 63
    The Pentecost Event and Its Significance 63
    A First Generation Summary 65

How We Got the Christian Bible 67
    The Meaning of "Canon" 67
    Our Approach in This Section 67
    Historical Origins 68
    The Sequence of the Production of the New Testament Documents 69
        I Thessalonians (AD 51-52) 69
        II Thessalonians (AD 52) 69
        Galatians (AD 54-55) 69
        I Corinthians (AD 54-56) 69
        II Corinthians (AD 57-58) 70
        Romans (AD 58-59) 70
        Philippians (AD 63-65) 70
        Ephesians (AD 63-65) 71
        Colossians (AD 63-65) 71
        Philemon (AD 63-65) 71
        Mark (before AD 65) 72

    Matthew (AD 75-90) 72
    Luke (generally dated AD 75-90 but I believe before AD 65) 72
    Acts (generally dated AD 80-90 but I believe before AD 65) 72
    John (AD 90-100) 73
    I & II Timothy and Titus 73
    Hebrews (before AD 70) 73
    James (after AD 65) 74
    I Peter (AD 60-64) 74
    II Peter (AD 90-110) 74
    I John (after AD 90) 74
    II & III John (after AD 90) 74
    Jude (after AD 100) 75
    Revelation (AD 95-100) 75
  Sifting and Sorting as Part of the Canonizing Process 75
  The Gathering and Evaluating Process 77

Major Developments in Traditional Christianity 81
  The First Shaping of Christian Doctrines 81
  The Period of the Early Councils 82
  The Establishment of a Hierarchical Church 83
  Division into Eastern and Western Churches 84
  The Dissenter Factor 84
  The Protestant Reformation 84

Seeking a Personal Faith 85
  A Summary of Some Traditional Beliefs 85
    People Are Created in the Image of God 85
    People Are Sinful 87
    The Consequences of Sinfulness 88
    What I Believe 90
    People Can Be Saved 90
    Fundamentals of Faith about Salvation 91
  What Does Salvation Mean, and How Are People Saved? 96
  The Question of Limited Atonement 97
  The Priesthood Question 99
  The "Covenant People" Question 100
  A Different Look at the Meaning of Salvation 101
  The Tragic Neglect of the Holy Spirit 105

A Presumptuous Criticism of Traditional Christianity 109
   The Role of Ritual Sacrifices 109
   The Doctrine and Practice of Baptism 111
   The Development of a Sacramental Priesthood 113
   Toward A Recovery of True Sacrament 117

Summary and Conclusion 119

Prologue

Religion is a human thing. It has to do with the supernatural, but in itself religion is a human experience. Religion is a personal response of trust in whatever is believed by a person to be of supreme value. Religious institutions such as churches, temples, synagogues, mosques and covens are pervasive throughout the world, but these institutions are not the essence of religion. They are organized channels for religious experience and expression. The fundamental nature of religion is a personal experience of a sense of supernatural value and authority, a belief in some force or being outside oneself that influences one's life and destiny.

A sense of the supernatural gives rise to an inner motivation to express that sense of something supernatural in outward ways, such as by some form of worship. Belief in some fate-controlling influence leads to attempts to appease or mollify that force or being. Religion, however, is always rooted in an individual person's experience or belief.

It is quite common for people to embrace a particular expression of religion through a presentation about that religion by another person. This is what happens when a person accepts a particular faith as a result of example and teaching by parents, through the teaching and preaching of a church or other religious organization, or in response to some other form of communication about religious beliefs. It is less common for people to seriously examine the foundations of their religious faith and the meaning of their religious practices.

Writings that are believed to be sacred play an important part in the way people understand religion. Through generations and centuries, records of the things believed in by the varied religions of humankind have been written and preserved. As these writings came to be considered sacred, they came to have great influence in the lives of people who believed and practiced each particular religion. Therefore, it is important to consider how the sacred books of the varied historic religions came into being and how they came to be considered sacred.

The purpose of this work is to encourage its readers to make a sincere effort to understand their personal faith. Such an effort is aided by a basic understanding of the historical origins and development of religious thought and expression. Sincere effort has been made to keep the language of this work non-technical. When theological or philosophical terms are used, they are explained as simply as possible. I hope that this work will be helpful to readers who are not familiar with the historical development of the religion in which they have placed personal faith. An elementary discussion of several historic religious faiths is included to help individuals compare their personal faith with the faiths and practices of others.

Since the origins of religious thought, faith and practice reach back to prehistoric and prescientific times, we must consider the influences of limited knowledge and superstition. And we will, of course, have to try to understand as many varieties of religious belief and practice as possible.

This writing is intended for Christian laypersons; therefore, it seems appropriate to affirm that I am a devout Christian and a practicing churchman whose deep conviction is that, in Jesus of Nazareth, the truest revelation of the nature of God, the character of God, and the meaning of religion has reached its highest expression.

Some Words about Words and Origins

Among Christians, the word god is universally used as if it were a proper name. This is technically incorrect, for the word god is a generic term referring to a supernatural and/or supreme being.[1] The English word *God* has essentially the same meaning as the Hebrew word *El* (plural *Elohim*) and the Arabic word *Allah*. These words all refer to a supreme being, but they do not in themselves describe the nature or character of that supreme being. The nature and character of *El* in Hebrew religion are reflected in the Hebrew Scriptures (the Old Testament of the Christian Bible) by the personal name *Yahweh* (*Jehovah*), after the experience of Moses on Mount Sinai (Exodus 3:13-15). The personal nature and character of *God* in the Christian religion is identified as *The Father of our Lord Jesus Christ*. There is no such personal name for the Supreme Being in Islam; Muslims simply use the generic term *Allah*.[2]

In the historical development of religious thought and expression, there has been a general movement from belief in many divine beings (polytheism) toward belief in one supreme divine being (monotheism). There is a theory that among primitive peoples there was a common belief in a distant High God who was the creator of the world and the parent of lesser deities who were believed to influence the daily lives of the people. This belief is similar to the Great Spirit (Great White Father) believed in by some Native American tribes. Those who find evidence of this original monotheism believe that it was corrupted into the animism and polytheism that were the predominant forms of primitive religion. True monotheism developed later.

Three great monotheistic religions are widely practiced in modern times: Judaism, Christianity and Islam. These religions, however, were relatively late in developing. Judaism is the oldest of the three, beginning with Abraham about 2100-2000 BC. Christianity had its beginning through the life and teachings of Jesus of Nazareth. Islam began through the writings and influence of Muhammed (AD 570-632).

There were great primitive religious systems that developed long before these three monotheistic religions. The following systems of worship developed earlier than Judaism:

- Sumerian sun, moon, air and water gods in Mesopotamia;
- Animal-headed gods in Egypt;
- Primitive religions in China centered on harmony between heaven, earth and humanity;
- Primitive religions in India embodying the doctrines of karma and transmigration;
- Tribal fertility religions in pre-Hebrew Canaan.

The following systems of religion developed in the eastern world after the beginning of Judaism but before the beginning of Christianity:

- Zoroastrianism in Persia, probably before 1000 BC;
- Shinto in Japan, about 600 BC;
- Buddhism in northern India, about 500 BC;
- Confucianism in China, about 500 BC.

Islam developed in Arabia and spread across North Africa some 600 years after the beginning of Christianity. The Greek and Roman pantheons (groups of deities that focused on natural forces and human emotions) developed as the Graeco-Roman cultures and empires rose and fell. As Christianity spread west through Europe and North America, it met and interacted with already existing forms of primitive and nature-oriented religions.

All of these religious systems were and are believed to be authentic and supremely valuable by those who have believed in them and practiced various expressions of them.

The Basis of Religious Beliefs

Systems of religion have arisen in two primary ways and can be described as *discovery religions* or *revealed religions*. *Discovery religions* are systems of religious practice developed by people who observe influences in nature that affect their lives, come to believe that those features or forces have supernatural powers, and fashion worship practices to seek to please them or to pacify their displeasure. *Revealed religions*, on the other hand, are systems of religious practice that are formed by people who are convinced that a supernatural person/power has made known to them, by a revelation, how they should live and give homage to the person/power doing the revealing. The difference is whether a system of religion has its origin from an *upward* human search or a *downward* supernatural revelation. The three great monotheistic religions (Judaism, Christianity and Islam) all affirm their origins as a revelation by a great, Supreme God. These are discussed in detail later. The other religious systems developed as *discovery religions* based on observation of controlling influences in nature or in human life.

All of these religious systems are human creations. They differ in origin on the basis of human conviction about what has supernatural influence, what is worthy of worship, and what calls for the commitment of a person's life. Religion is about the supernatural, but religious convictions, practices and systems are human responses to human beliefs about the supernatural.

In examining religious beliefs and practices, the three most important factors to try to understand are the nature of the supernatural person/power being worshipped, the character of that person/power, and the relationship of human persons to that supernatural person/power.

With these basic propositions set forth, we will now examine the origin and development of various religious systems to demonstrate how these ideas play out.

[1] Merriam-Webster, *Collegiate Dictionary*, 10th ed., (Springfield, Massachusets, 1999), 500.
[2] Edward Jurji, "Allah," *Collier's Encyclopedia*, 1 (1987): 570.

Religion among Primitive Peoples

Anthropologists study the origin and development of human cultures. Archaeologists study the material that past human cultures have left behind. These two groups of specialists agree that there is evidence of religious systems from as early as 20,000 years ago, ages before the times of Abraham, Jesus and Muhammed. The most ancient evidence is mainly items buried with people and markings on cave walls. The things they valued and tried to preserve help us to understand how they thought and the things they worshipped.

It is an interesting experience to reflect and wonder about the questions that arose in the minds of prehistoric people. These were people who were still learning by observation about the changing of the seasons and the dependable movements of the stars and planets. What would you and I have thought about the sun and the moon if we had not known that one was a star and the other a satellite of the earth? What did the first people who dwelt on seashores think as they tried to understand the daily rise and fall of the ocean's surface? Imagine how the ancients tried to figure out why seeds sprouted to become new plants and grow new seeds. They did not have a massive storehouse of accumulated knowledge and experience to explain these natural phenomena as we did from our earliest childhood. So a very normal reaction on their part was to be overwhelmed, awed, and often fearful of these features of nature that they saw all around them.

Consequently, as they faced questions they could not answer, they searched for explanations. One of the ways they accounted for these natural phenomena was to fashion an idea of some supernatural power that controlled things they could not understand, explain or control.

Early in the development of human cultures there arose the belief that special powers, something more than human, resided in certain people, such as tribal chiefs, medicine men and magicians. These people were believed to control forces in the unseen world which responded only to them. Consequently, the rest of the group held them in awe and, often, in fear. An aura of mystery surrounded these people, which in turn became a source of their influence and control over their tribal groups. Their display of "powers" was how they got to be tribal chiefs, medicine men and magicians.

At one time or another, among one primitive group or another, almost every animal or plant or natural object has had ascribed to it an active spirit that influenced and controlled some aspect of life. The productivity of fields, the virility of herds, and the fertility of women were all believed to be controlled by spirits that resided in natural objects, such as rocks or trees or streams of water.

Religious systems arose around beliefs that supernatural spirits dwelt in various objects. Religious practices developed through which people expressed homage to those spirits they believed in and from which they hoped to receive favorable treatment. As human cultures became more highly developed, their religious systems became more focused on specific objects of deification. This gave rise to a stage in religious thought called polytheism, the belief in the existence of many gods. We turn now to an examination of some examples of religious systems and practices that predate the beginning of Judaism, the first of the monotheistic religions.

Pre-Monotheistic Religions in Asia

Mesopotamia

In the centuries before 2000 BC, both culture and religion were developing among the Sumerian peoples in the region called Mesopotamia that lay between the Tigris and Euphrates rivers. Human culture developed as the more primitive hunters and fishers gathered into villages, often for protection, and rules for living together became necessary. Along with more organized culture, religious practices also began to take on order. The mystic powers that appeared to be present in natural forces were given names:[1]

- Babbar the sun-god
- Sin the moon-god
- Enlil the air-god
- Ea the water-god

Each of these deities was identified with one of the major cities. For example, Sin, the moon-god, was primarily identified with and worshipped at the city of Ur, from which Abraham migrated to begin the Semitic religion of Judaism. These various deities were believed to be hospitable toward each other and not competitive. Later, the worship of the goddess Ishtar developed. She was believed to be the mother-goddess and the goddess of fertility. As such, she gave children to women, young to animals, and life to vegetation. It is easy to see why she was the focus of so much adoration and homage. In the minds of the masses, she was immediately associated with those basic concerns of everyday life.

> The name "Sin" is not to be confused with the concept of sin as moral evil in the Hebrew and Christian religions.

When Babylon became a great city and King Hammurabi established his reign over most of Mesopotamia (sometime between 2100 BC and 1700 BC), Marduk, the god of that city, was believed to have taken over the functions of all the surrounding gods and was worshipped among the Sumerians as the lord of the heavens.

These Sumerian ideas and practices were based on beliefs that supernatural divine powers were present in natural objects such as the sun, moon, air and water. These beliefs resulted from the influence of those natural objects on people's lives. Remember that they were living in the pre-scientific age, more than 3,000 years before Copernicus (AD 1500) established that the earth rotates in an orbit around the sun instead of the sun circling the earth every day. This was also long before Galileo (AD 1600) made his contributions to the basic beginnings of the science of physics, and before Isaac Newton (AD 1700) defined the basic laws of gravity and motion. Their understanding of the divine was of an impersonal power rather than a personal God. Their religious practices were intended to engender favorable treatment by those supernatural forces, not to become like the divine force they worshipped.

The development of religious beliefs and practices in Mesopotamia is especially important for Jews and Christians. Abraham's sense of a divine call to leave his culture and religious environment to make a new start, develop a new family tradition, and practice a religion based on a covenant with a Supreme God reflects his awareness of the inadequacy of the nature and fertility religions of Mesopotamia. Abraham acted out of a conviction that he had received a revelation from that Supreme God.

The Ancient Religions of Canaan

When Abraham arrived in Canaan sometime around 2000 BC, he found the land inhabited by several Semitic tribes who were primarily worshippers of Baals. The Baals were nature and fertility deities believed to be spirits that inhabited natural objects such as trees or boulders. These deities were believed to be local manifestations of the "great sky-god Baal," who was believed to control the weather. The local Baals were believed to give or withhold the fertility of fields, animals and people.[2]

Their religious practices were primarily agricultural festivals, animal sacrifices, and offerings of harvest first fruits. There were also perversions of basic Baalism by practices of child sacrifice and sacred prostitution by vestal virgins at their altars.

The Religions of India

In primitive times (before 2000 BC), the predominant people of India were ancestors of the dark-skinned Dravidians, who are still found in the southern half of the subcontinent. They left no writings, but archaeological remains reflect a well-developed culture and religion. The primitive religion included some indications of belief in later concepts, such as the transmigration of souls through successive reincarnations.[3]

As the Hebrew religion was emerging in Canaan, significant and widely influential religious developments were taking place in ancient India from 2000 to 1000 BC. Waves of Aryans migrated from the areas of ancient Persia. They brought with them beliefs in polytheistic religion based on the worship of nature deities that were personifications of natural forces such as sun, moon and storm.

As the migrating Aryans intermingled with the native Dravidians, their cultures and religions influenced each other, and from 1500 to 800 BC the highly complex Vedic religion developed. The religious writings of the period, called Vedas, reflect a mixture of nature worship, moral guidance, magic and medicinal arts.

The struggle between the Aryan and non-Aryan cultures led to the development of distinct social groups (nobles, priests, peasants and slaves), which in turn developed into a rigid caste system. These caste distinctions, through the social struggle for status and control, came to have religious as well as cultural importance.[4]

During the next period (down to about 300 BC), a very philosophical approach to religion in India developed. This searching after the nature of reality was given expression in writings called Upanishads. These became the fourth section of each of the Vedas from earlier times. A wide diversity of thought was present among the thinkers and schools of thought, but there was agreement about the central belief that all being is grounded in a single reality called Brahma, which is infinite in essence and is self-sufficient, but indefinable.

Another development of the speculative philosophy of that same period was belief in reincarnation (or the transmigration of souls). This belief goes thus: At death a soul does not pass into permanent residence in heaven or hell, but is reborn in another state of existence either higher or lower than in the previous life. The nature of the next birth was believed to be determined by what was called the Law of Karma. The word karma means "deeds" or "works." The Law of Karma was that a person's deeds had the consequence of determining the state of that person's next existence.

Not only was reincarnation the fate of individual persons, but time itself was believed to move through succeeding cycles. The world decays and dissolves, and all souls enter a suspended state. After the world rests awhile, it comes to life again, and the souls take up new bodies and new lives.

A deep sense of fated determinism developed in the psyche of masses in India, leading to profound depressions and a yearning for a way of release. Out of this search for a different hope developed two new religious systems of belief.

Jainism and Buddhism

Deep yearning for a release from endless reincarnations led to the rise of Jainism during the sixth century BC. Basic to Jainism is the belief that any person of any caste can achieve release from the fate of reincarnation by personal accomplishment rather than by offering sacrifices to the gods. This personal achievement would be primarily by asceticism (that is, by self-denial of pleasures and bodily satisfactions), which if practiced sufficiently would enable a person to be released into Nirvana. Nirvana was believed to be an unconscious state of total unity with and absorption into Brahma, which was believed to be the reality of everything that exists. For example, being released into Nirvana would be like dropping a drop of water into the ocean, where it would completely lose its identity and become a part of the whole.

Jainism expanded the traditional concern for cattle as sacred to hold that all forms of life are sacred and are to be preserved wherever and whenever possible. These beliefs placed such rigorous demands on people that the multitudes did not accept them. Consequently, Jainism never became a mass movement, although it is still practiced by a minority of people in India.

Buddhism also developed in India during the same time period. Its founder was Siddhartha Gautama, who lived from 560 to 480 BC. (These are legendary dates and are not certain.) After years of disillusionment, Gautama abandoned his family and went searching for meaning in life through severe self-denial. Finally, in abject defeat, he sat under a fig tree (later called a *"bo"* tree) and vowed to remain there until enlightenment came to him. He was afterward called Buddha, "the enlightened one." His "enlightenment" came in the form of conviction that human well-being could be achieved by following a "noble Eightfold Way." The eight principles are: right views, right intentions, right speech, right action, right livelihood, right effort, right mindfulness and right concentration.

This concept is clearly more a philosophy of life than faith in a deity to be worshipped.

There is no indication that Gautama intended to form a new religion. He was a practicing Hindu, but as he applied his understanding of a noble Way he changed his teachings about religion. His basic modifications of traditional Hinduism were:

- He focused primarily on vital human issues (more like psychology than philosophy).
- He rejected religious devotion as a way of salvation and considered prayer as of no avail.
- He taught that the soul does not exist. Human personality is made up of body, feelings, understanding, will and consciousness. This personality is bound up in endless reincarnations.
- He sought enlightenment and freedom from sensual yearnings so that he might be free from desires and experience an earthly foretaste of Nirvana.

Buddhism, like Jainism, rejected the ascetic rigors of the Vedas and offered a way of salvation based on individual effort and achievement. Buddhism, unlike traditional Hinduism, developed a missionary spirit and spread to many other southeastern Asian countries. At the same time Hinduism was recovering its predominant place in India, and Buddhism was overshadowed and pushed aside.[5] More about Buddhism later.

Classical and Modern Hinduism

Hinduism developed through the centuries and, through competitive interchange with other religious movements, became the dominant religion of India. Its most classical statement in sacred literature is an epic poem, the *Bhagavad Gita*. This poem is made up of stories about the struggles of heroes and deities that give expression to the basic philosophy and religious beliefs of Hinduism. The basic teachings of the Bhagavad Gita are:

1. Each person has an obligation to be obedient and fulfill the requirements of one's caste.
2. Release from endless reincarnations can be achieved by anyone through self-denial, meditation, devotion to the gods, or faithfulness to one's caste.
3. The god Vishnu cares enough about humans that he at times takes on various forms to aid humans in their struggles.

Hinduism continued to develop and change after its classical period, which ended in the early centuries of the Christian era. While the belief in the existence and influence of many deities has continued in Hinduism, much of its focus has come to center on three major gods:

- Brahma, believed to be the creator of the world;
- Shiva, believed to be the god of disease, death and destruction;
- Vishnu, believed to be the god of benevolence, love and forgiveness

Because Hindus worship many deities, there are many religious festivals and pilgrimages practiced by various Hindu groups. As Hindus have traveled and migrated in modern times, Hinduism has come to be practiced primarily in small to medium-sized groups. It continues to be the major religion of India.

Through the 4,000 years of Hebrew and Christian history to date, Hindu religious beliefs and practices have evolved and changed. The concept of deity has become more personal, as in ascribing personal characteristics to Brahma, Vishnu and Shiva. However, religious benefits for the individual are still believed to be the result of individual achievements through self-discipline, asceticism and caste faithfulness.[6]

The Religions of China

Ancient Chinese culture (before the eleventh century BC) was characterized by the worship of many deities which were believed to control the natural universe. Ritual sacrifices were a pervasive expression of the Chinese people's reverence for these gods, and such sacrifices were offered regularly, especially seasonally, in an effort to gain benefit and avoid harm.

Reverence for parents and ancestors has from antiquity been a predominant feature of Chinese life and culture. As a result, "old age" is the ultimate term of respect. There is such a religious quality to Chinese expressions of respect that it is usually referred to as ancestor worship.

During the 900s BC the Chou dynasty decreed that there was one Supreme God (Shang Ti) who controlled the universe, rewarded morality and punished immorality. This period is thought to closely parallel the development of Hebrew monotheism. The royal decree, however, never gained enough popular following to become a major religious development.

During the sixth century BC and afterward, Taoism and Confucianism developed as two philosophies-religions (more philosophies than religions). They became the dominant influences in the realm of morality and religion.[7]

Lao-tzu was the legendary founder of Taoism. Tradition holds that he was born in 604 BC (or 570 BC). There is a disputed tradition that he wrote his teachings in the document TaoTeChing (the way of nature), which became the sacred book of Taoism. From the perspective of religious thought, Taoism is more a philosophy of life to be followed than a religion to be practiced.[8]

Confucius lived from 551 to 479 BC. He was primarily a scholar and teacher. While he was not an atheist, he believed and taught that religion was inconsequential. His teachings were collected by followers after his death in a document called the Analects of Confucius. This document has been described as, and is widely considered to be, the most influential work in Chinese literature. The teachings of Confucius are more a philosophy than a theology, for he was primarily concerned with the nature of human society and a system of ethics.[9]

Buddhism in China

The Buddhist religion began in India during the sixth century BC as the followers of Gautama, "the enlightened one," took the principles of his "noble Eightfold Way," made them into religious precepts, and elevated him to the status of deity (see pages 9-10).

Buddhism migrated to the north into the closed and isolated culture of China at about the time of the beginning of the Christian era. The Buddhists brought monks and monasteries to China and introduced them into the culture. In China, the religion of Buddhism competed with Confucianism and Taoism for the minds and hearts of the people. With its more distinctly religious practices, Buddhism became the most purely religious system in China.[10]

Shinto, the Religion of Japan

Shinto is the native religion of Japan and has been practiced there primarily. While Shinto is practiced as a religion, it is essentially a system of reverent patriotism more than of divine worship.

The traditions of Shinto began with belief in nature deities who were thought to have created the islands of Japan and ruled over the people who inhabited those islands. The traditions that developed included belief that the Japanese people were descended from the deities.

Over the centuries, the Shinto traditions developed into a hybrid mix of nature worship and ancestor worship. Shinto, as a native religion, identified with the specific geography and people of Japan and developed into a state religion with an emperor who was believed to be divine.

Shinto was practiced in Japan as a state religion in a closed, isolated society until the mid-twentieth century AD. Expanding world trade and World War II ended the cultural isolation of Japan and caused Shinto to become more familiar to the rest of the world.[11]

Zoroastrianism in Persia

One of the least known of ancient religions is Zoroastrianism, which developed in Persia and has continued to be primarily a Persian religion, with a small following in Iran. It is probably, however, the most important ancient religion for Judaism and Christianity because of its influence on the Hebrew captives in Babylon/Persia during the sixth and fifth centuries BC.

There is a great deal of uncertainty about the origins of Zoroastrianism. Little is known about the life of Zarathustra (later known as Zoroaster), the founder of this philosophy and religion, although legends survived about him. The dates of his life have been variously reported to be between 1400 and 600 BC. He is generally believed to have lived before 1000 BC.

Before the time of Zoroaster's life, the religions of the Persian people were primarily focused on belief in supernatural powers in sun, moon, earth, fire and water. Above these local deities they believed in a Supreme Lord, *Ahura Mazda* (Persian for Wise Lord), a highly ethical deity.[12]

Zoroaster believed and declared that angels came to him and told him that Ahura Mazda was the only true god and that Zoroaster was to be his prophet. He declared that this god manifested himself in human life through "the agency of six modes"—knowledge, love, service, piety, wholeness and immortality.

The most distinctive contribution to religious thought made by Zoroaster was probably his understanding and teaching about evil. Before Zoroaster, most religious understanding about good and evil focused on *moral monism*—that is, the belief that there is one source of both good and bad. Ancient people believed that good came to them by the favor of the deity they worshipped and obeyed, and bad came to them if they were unfaithful in devotion or disobedient and thus incurred the disfavor of the god. Zoroaster came to the belief that good and bad do not emerge from the same source. He developed this belief in *moral dualism* and taught that the source of good influence and blessing was Ahura Mazda. He identified the source of evil influence and bad effects as Angra Mainyu (the evil spirit), later to be known as Shaitin (or Satan). In order not to violate his belief in one god (monotheism), Zoroaster described the evil spirit as existing under the supreme sovereignty of the one Supreme God (that is, as a "demigod," or in later Hebrew belief "a fallen angel.")

Zoroaster also believed and taught that people have freedom of choice, not a fated determinism, in how they respond to good and evil and how they live their lives. This belief was also reflected in his understanding of the destiny of people. He set forth the ideas of paradise (a place of beauty and pleasantness) and hell (a place of torment) to which people went after a general resurrection and judgment. According to Zoroaster, each person's final destiny is determined by the moral decisions of good or evil made as they exercised their free choices in their lives. This was a significantly different understanding of destiny than the Hebrew belief in *sheol*, the place in the center of the earth where the dead go and gradually fade into nothingness. It is also different from belief in reincarnation and transmigration, that at death people are reborn in another state of existence either higher or lower than in the previous life depending on the moral quality of their previous life.[13]

As we try to understand the influence of Zoroastrianism on Hebrew religion or their influence on each other, it is important to take into account the historic context and the stage of religious understanding present at the time. By the sixth century BC, leaders among the Hebrews who returned from Persia were firmly monotheistic (assuming that chapters 40-66 of the Isaiah document are post-exilic, see Isaiah 44:9-17). If Zoroaster lived before 1000 BC, then Zoroastrianism would have had a monotheistic influence on the Hebrews while they were in Babylon and Persia. The documents of the Hebrew Old Testament, which had their origins in the oral and written traditions that preceded the Babylonian exile, do not refer to Satan and do not reflect the moral dualism that was present in Zoroaster's teaching. The documents that come out of post-exilic Judaism do have several such references. Religious ideas such as freedom of moral choice, the influence of an evil demigod, an eschatological end of the world, resurrection of the body, and paradise or hell as individual destiny, were all themes of Zoroastrianism and had become established tenets of Judaism by the end of the BC era.

In the history of the period, the Persian Empire failed in its attempts to spread westward into Europe. Instead, the Greek Empire rose to prominence (after 350 BC) and the armies of Alexander the Great overwhelmed the Persian Empire. This likely was a primary obstacle preventing Zoroastrianism from becoming a major religion in pre-Christian Europe.

[1] John B. Noss, *Man's Religions* (New York: The Macmillan Company, 1960), 60.
[2] Norman H. Snaith, "Exegesis of I Kings," *The Interpreter's Bible*, 3 (1954): 153.
[3] Noss, *Man's Religions*, 114. Lewis M. Hopfe and Mark R. Woodard, Religions of the World, 9th ed. (Upper Saddle River NJ: Pearson/Prentice Hall, 2005), 76-77.
[4] Hopfe and Woodard, *Religions of the World*, 76-77. Noss, "Man's Religions," 115-116.
[5] Hopfe and Woodard, *Religions of the World*, 88-89.
[6] Hopfe and Woodward, *Religions of the World*, 101-102, 106-107.
[7] Geoffrey Parrinder, ed., *World Religions* (New York: Facts on File Publications, 1971), 304-306. Hopfe and Woodward, *Religions of the World*, 169-173.
[8] Hopfe and Woodward, *Religions of the World*, 175-177.
[9] Noss, Man's Religions, 339-344. Hopfe and Woodward, *Religions of the World*, 183-188.
[10] Parrinder, *World Religions*, 343-344.
[11] Noss, *Man's Religions*, 399-404. Hopfe and Woodward, *Religions of the World*, 203-210.
[12] Hopfe and Woodward, *Religions of the World*, 221-224.
[13] Hopfe and Woodward, *Religions of the World*, 224-230. Parrinder, World Religions, 177-178. Noss, *Man's Religions*, 440-446.

The Rise of Monotheistic and Revealed Religions

The three major systems of religion which are based on belief in a Supreme Personal God are Hebrew/Judaism, Christianity and Islam. They arose and developed in that historical order. Each of these religions is practiced across broad portions of the world. Their expansion came about almost universally in modern times due to the globalizing of travel, migration, commerce and communication.

Hebrew Religion/Judaism

The Hebrew religion had its origin with the migration of Abram (Abraham) from Chaldea in Mesopotamia to Canaan/Palestine about 2000 BC. His migration is described in the Hebrew Scriptures (Genesis 12 and following) as resulting from a sense of revelation and calling from a Supreme God, who was not the Moon God predominantly worshipped in the Sumerian culture of Chaldea.[1]

Abraham's arrival in Canaan began a period of patriarchal clan life and nomadic herding in that area that lasted for three generations. Religion during that period was primarily devotion to a clan deity, based on a covenant relationship in which the deity and the people belonged to each other. The patriarchal period ended when a famine resulted in the Hebrew migration from Canaan to settle in Egypt under the leadership of Joseph, son of Jacob and great-grandson of Abraham.

After generations of prosperous living in an area of the Nile River delta, the Hebrews became so large a group that the Egyptians feared their disloyalty in case of war. So they reduced the Hebrews to a condition of slavery. Under the leadership of Moses, the Hebrews escaped their bondage and migrated into the Sinai Peninsula. They were convinced that their freedom had come as a miraculous deliverance by their God, and their celebration of their exodus became a central feature of their religious faith and their festivals from that time onward.[2]

The escaped slaves (traditionally numbered at 300,000) were essentially an unorganized group with some sense of family identity as descendants of the twelve sons of Jacob (later named Israel). Moses led them to a mountain where he had experienced a sense of religious calling (the burning bush incident) and a conviction that their God had revealed himself as YaHWeH (the Great "I Am" of Exodus 3:14-15). The people camped in the Sinai area while Moses spent time on the mountain communing with their God. During this period, Moses began to develop an organized structure for the life of the children of Israel. According to the traditions recorded in the Hebrew Scriptures, Moses set forth civil laws to guide the people in their relationships with one another, moral laws to guide their conduct, dietary laws to guide their health habits, and sacrificial laws to guide their religious practices. All of these laws were set forth as ways the Hebrews could obey God and be faithful to their covenant with him.

After the period in Sinai, the Hebrews set out to migrate to what they considered their ancestral home in Canaan, an area they believed their God had given them as a homeland. Arriving on the southern border, they halted, fearing that they could not conquer and displace the inhabitants. They turned back into the Sinai desert (the wilderness) and spent a nomadic generation there before attempting again to migrate into Canaan. After that generation had died, the Hebrews skirted around Canaan into Moab, across the Jordan River just east of the lower Jordan and the Dead Sea. Moses died there, and Joshua became the leader of the people.

Some of the Hebrews chose to settle on the lands east of the Jordan. But ten of the twelve clan families under the leadership of Joshua set out to cross the Jordan, destroy or drive out the inhabitants there, and take possession of the land. The situation was entirely different from that which existed when Abraham first came to Canaan. Then, the Hebrews were only a nomadic group of less than fifty people, wandering about to find grazing for their herds. They were readily tolerated, and little conflict arose. When Joshua came with an invading army of thousands, determined to claim all the land in the name of the Hebrew God, the Canaanite inhabitants knew that their lives and families were gravely threatened, and so they fought fiercely. This ancient attempt at ethnic cleansing by Joshua and the Hebrew army was only partially successful. The tribal inhabitants were farmers who fought fiercely to hold and protect their lands. The Hebrews, whose heritage was that of nomadic herdsmen, had to settle for the more mountainous areas, which were quite suitable for grazing. The result was that the Hebrews and Canaanites continued to live in adjacent areas with times of tolerance, times of pirating raids on each other, and times of outright warfare. Neither could completely vanquish the other. (This period is described in the books of Joshua and Judges of the Hebrew Scriptures).[3]

The situation led the Hebrews to decide they needed to have a king over all their tribes who could raise an army strong enough to totally subdue the Canaanites. Their first king was Saul, whose task it became to bring the tribes together with enough acceptance of his leadership that they could become a nation. The second king was David, who successfully strengthened and expanded the Hebrew nation. His reign was later considered by the Hebrews to be their "golden age." The third king was Solomon, son of David, who was so ambitious and of such an imperial spirit that he made a great name for himself. Solomon, however, caused such burdens on the people by his egotism and ambitious imperial projects that after his death a rebellion split the Hebrews into two kingdoms.

The kingdoms existed alongside each other for about two centuries, sometimes at peace and sometimes at war, sometimes making alliances with each other and sometimes making alliances with neighboring kingdoms against each other.

In the late eighth century BC, the Assyrian empire conquered the Northern Kingdom (Israel), took the leadership captive into Assyria, and brought in Assyrians to keep the conquered nation under control. These became the "Ten Lost Tribes of Israel." A great deal of intermarriage took place, and the people of the area became a mixed-race people (the Samaritans described in the Hebrew books of Ezra and Nehemiah).

The Southern Kingdom (Judah) continued to exist with some degree of independence for another century, during which the Assyrian empire declined and the Babylonian empire rose to predominance. In the early sixth century BC, the Babylonian empire conquered the Southern Kingdom, devastated the city of Jerusalem, destroyed Solomon's Temple, and took a large percentage of the inhabitants into captivity. In large measure, this was the end of a truly identifiable Hebrew nation until the establishment of the modern nation of Israel following the conclusion of World War II.

After the Persian Empire conquered the Babylonian Empire in the late sixth century (BC), the Hebrew captives were freed to return to Canaan. Over the next generation, remnant groups did return and re-established themselves in the Judean area. They built a small temple in Jerusalem and rebuilt some of the city and its walls. They made their homes there, but they remained a subject people, dominated by the marching armies and the ebb and flow of nations around them.

The history of the rise and fall of the Hebrews as a national group also included the development of the Hebrew religion from the simple covenant of Abraham to the complex institution of Judaism by the time of the beginning of Christianity. Some of those developing features are important to understanding Hebrew religion, the Old Testament of the Christian Bible, and some of the tenets of the Christian religion.

The sense of covenant between Abraham and God as reflected in Genesis 12:1-3 included the following features: Abraham was to migrate away from his family and the moon-worship culture of Chaldea and go to a new place to which God would lead him. Abraham believed that God would bless him to become a respected person and head of a large nation, and that God would be with him during any conflicts. And Abraham believed God wanted to use him as an instrument to reveal God to the nations and bring God's blessings to all the people of the world. Abraham was one of the great spiritual giants of human history, and his sense of a revealed covenant from God was a major leap in the development of religious thought and practice.

The Hebrew Scriptures of the Old Testament reflect that the mass of the Hebrew people embraced the parts of the covenant that dealt with their enlargement, their privileges and their prosperity. They, did not, however, so freely embrace the idea of being a source of benefit and service to others. They developed into an exclusive society, believing that God cared much for them and little for all non-Hebrews.

Hebrew religion, as described in the Hebrew Scriptures, experienced significant developmental changes during the fifteen centuries from the migration of Abraham to Canaan until the return of the remnant groups from Babylon/Persia. The most significant formulation of Hebrew religious practices came out of the leadership of Moses following the Sinai period after the exodus from Egypt. The establishment of an official priesthood and an extensive sacrificial system became the most prominent features of Hebrew religious practices. These practices were centered in the mobile tabernacle during the wilderness era and later in Solomon's Temple after Jerusalem became the established center of Hebrew life and religion.

A major addition to Hebrew religious practice probably occurred during the Babylonian captivity after the temple was destroyed and the captives were separated from the religious roots of their homeland.[4] The synagogue became a major institution for preserving devotion to the Torah and faithfulness to the covenant with YaHWeH. Whereas the temple had been a center of ritual sacrifice, the synagogue developed as a center of teaching and disciplining. After the temple was rebuilt by the returning remnant from Babylon/Persia, and again built on a grander scale by Herod the Great, both temple and synagogue were prominent Jewish religious institutions when Jesus lived.

Historically, the Hebrews thought of David's reign as their "golden age" as a people and a nation. Consequently, as they declined as two divided nations to the time of Assyrian conquest of the Northern Kingdom and the Babylonian conquest of the Southern Kingdom, there arose among them the dream of a messianic age. They longed for a time when God would raise up and anoint from the descendants of David a new king who would lead a victorious army to throw off all adversaries and oppressors and raise the Hebrew nation to the golden age again.[5]

After centuries of hated submission to the Greek and Roman empires, the hope of a messianic age to restore them to exclusive prominence and prosperity was deeply embedded in the Jews of the first century among whom Jesus lived. It is easy to find traces of these Hebrew beliefs carried over and continued in the Christian religion as it developed.

Much of Hebrew religion focused on an exclusive relationship with God and was centered in conceited theocratic nationalism. There were, however, also great spiritual giants:
- Isaiah, who proclaimed the absolute truth of monotheism;
- Amos, who declared that God is on the side of justice;

- Micah, who understood that we are not made right with God by animal sacrifice and burnt offerings but by embracing our humble relationship with the infinite sovereignty of God and by living out the values of kindness and mercy.

These inspired insights were where Hebrew religion truly foreshadowed the fuller revelation that God would make through incarnation in Jesus of Nazareth.

Let it be said forthrightly that I do not for a moment think that those ancient men arrived at these ideas by their own rational acumen. I am convinced, without any doubt, that the infinite eternal God has been forever, and always is, present with every living person. And I am convinced that this ever-present God has been, from the beginning, as the human species has evolved and developed, actively seeking to inspire and help every person to grasp a fuller understanding of the nature of God. And I am further convinced that it is the desire of this loving and compassionate God that every person will make a genuine faith commitment to a life of harmonious fellowship with God in the ideals which Jesus referred to as "abundant life."

God was able to bring to pass, through Hebrew religion, significant advances in the way people understood the nature of God and what it meant to live in harmony with God. Later, God chose personal involvement to advance his eternal purposes through incarnation. This is the wonderful story of Christianity.

Christianity

Christianity had its origin through the life and ministry of Jesus of Nazareth. We are not certain about the exact dates of Jesus' life. Our BC/AD dates were not established until AD 525, when a monk and mathematician named Dennis the Short calculated the time of Jesus' birth in relation to events in the Roman calendar and called that date *Anno Domini* 1 (the year of our Lord). The notes by which he made his calculations did not survive, so we do not know how he arrived at the date. Many other ancient astronomers and mathematicians and historians tried to establish the date of the birth of Jesus using Roman history and the dates of eclipses and stellar events. Opinions as to the exact date still vary; however, there is general agreement that Jesus was born before AD 1, sometime between BC 6 and BC 2.[6]

Let me at this point state that I have not written this part of the historical account based on my Christian faith. This is an attempt to describe events in the life of Jesus as they would have been seen and understood by a non-committed observer. The meaning of the life of Jesus will be the subject for consideration later.

Two major accounts of the birth of Jesus in Bethlehem in Judea have survived in Christian tradition in the Gospels of Matthew and Luke. These stories were preserved in oral tradition until the Gospel records were written some two generations later.

Jesus lived in comparative isolation with his family in Nazareth for thirty years. He then spent three to four years in public ministry. His active ministry was primarily teaching and responding to human needs among the common people. Strong traditions have held that he did many miraculous things, like feeding multitudes from little food, healing illnesses, restoring sight to blind persons, and even restoring to life some who had died.

Jesus gathered around him a group of twelve followers who came to be known as "disciples" (learners) or "apostles" (persons sent out on a mission), or simply as "The Twelve." This group went about with Jesus throughout his public ministry. They were witnesses to his death, and they became the first witnesses of the belief that he was a divine messiah.

Because there was a great and widespread yearning for a messianic deliverer from the hated Roman occupation, on several occasions crowds came to believe that Jesus just might be the "anointed one," and rumblings of a messianic revolution began to stir. Jesus always "damped down" those stirrings and tried repeatedly to help the people understand that he was not that kind of representative of God.

Throughout his years of public ministry, Jesus encountered resistance from the religious and civic leaders of the Jews. The occupying Roman officials essentially ignored Jesus. It was the practice of the powers in Rome to allow local leaders in the occupied regions to manage civil and religious affairs as long as they maintained order and collected the required taxes. The local leaders distrusted Jesus because of his influence among the crowds. They feared that he would create disorder and threaten their positions of favor with the Romans. The Jewish religious leaders violently disagreed with Jesus, both because he was teaching and practicing a different approach to religion than the one in which they were steeped and because his popularity among the masses threatened their positions of leadership as the priests and rabbis of Judaism.

As the religious leaders' struggles against Jesus became more intense, the Gospels record that he left Jerusalem and Galilee with his twelve closest followers to prepare them for the ministry they would lead after his departure. Passages in the Gospels reflect that the disciples were growing in their commitment to Jesus as a divine incarnation (Son of God) but still could not grasp many of his words, which were so radically different from all they had previously been taught to believe.

Jesus finally made a deliberate decision to go to Jerusalem and face the opposition against him there. His entry into the city at the beginning of Passover week was clearly understood by the crowd to be a messianic demonstration. Jesus made a definite declaration, however, that he was not there to lead a military rebellion. He rode into the city on a donkey, an established symbol of coming in peace. The Jewish leaders conspired to kill him to eliminate the thorn in their flesh that he had become and end his blasphemous influence on followers of their religion. The

Romans maintained their normal alert against any uprising and disorder during the major Jewish festival.

Jesus had enough insight to understand the threat to his life. He spent a farewell evening with his twelve disciples and then went out to Gethsemane on the Mount of Olives to wait for his enemies to do their treacherous work. His location was betrayed by Judas, one of his disciples. He was arrested and tried in a "kangaroo court" by the Jewish leaders who were convinced he was guilty of the religious offense of blasphemy and who had already decided on their verdict. They wanted him dead, but they were not permitted by the Roman occupiers to execute criminals themselves. They had to petition the Roman governor to condemn and execute.

When the Jewish leaders took Jesus before Pilate to request his execution, they changed their charge. They knew the Romans would not care about their religious quarrel, so they charged Jesus with insurrection. They said that he was claiming to be a king, which was treason against the emperor. When they were not able to convince Pilate that Jesus represented any such danger of insurrection, they resorted to intimidation. They threatened to report Pilate to the emperor for permitting a rebel to be active as a traitor to Roman authority and good order. Pilate let them have their way and had Jesus executed by crucifixion.

Some of Jesus' followers, with Pilate's permission, placed him in a temporary tomb. Two days later, his followers began to experience a series of events that persuaded them that he had risen from the dead and was alive again among them. Forty days later, they experienced an event that persuaded them that he had ascended into heaven and departed from their presence.

The development of the Christian church with its doctrines, rituals and practices is the focus of much of the rest of this volume. First, however, we will give attention to the origins of the third great monotheistic religion.

Islam, the Muslim Religion

Muhammad, the founder of Islam, lived from AD 570 to 632. He was a native of Mecca in Arabia. His tribe controlled the Ka'Ba, a religious shrine built around a meteorite they considered sacred. It was a center of polytheistic beliefs and rituals. Mecca was on the trade routes from the Indian Ocean to the Mediterranean Sea. As a youth, Muhammad was exposed to the caravans and the cultures and religions of the people who traveled with them. It seems evident that Muhammad thus became familiar with the religious beliefs of the Jews—that they were God's chosen and exclusively favored people through Abraham and the Isaac and Jacob line of his descendants. Muhammad and the Arabian tribes were descendants of Abraham through the Ishmael and Esau lines. Muhammad evidently reacted to the Hebrew claims of God's exclusive embrace of the Isaac and Jacob line with a "'t'aint so" attitude. After all, Ishmael was the firstborn son of Abraham and Esau was the firstborn son of Isaac.[7]

When he was twenty-five, Muhammad married a wealthy widow who owned a caravan. Her wealth enabled him to spend his time in meditation, pondering the fate of his people. During those periods of meditation, he claimed he received visits from an angel who revealed to him the text of the Golden Koran, the perfect word of Allah (God) in heaven. Muhammad claimed the angel enabled him to memorize the revelations accurately and completely, word for word, and to transcribe them as the Koran to be used by Allah's people on earth. Thus Islam, the Muslim religion, began.[8]

Islam had a slow beginning, but a period of nationalism developed and Islam swept with the Arab armies through much of the Middle East and North Africa. The Arab armies advanced west into Spain and as far as Tours in central France. In AD 732 they were turned back at the Battle of Tours. Europe continued to be primarily Christian, while Islam continued to be a major religion in Africa and Asia.

Islam is a strictly monotheistic religion. The Arabic word for "Supreme Being" is *Allah*, and Muslims use that word as their name for God. They believe that Allah is the same "one God" as the YaHWeH of Hebrew religion and the God of Christianity, but they claim that Judaism and Christianity have corrupted the religion of God and that Islam as revealed in the Koran is the only true religion. In this, as in every consideration about religion, I am convinced that the heart of every religion depends on the nature and character of God as understood and believed by the followers of that religion. *And* both Judaism and Islam include and proclaim things about the nature and character of God that are quite different from the nature and character revealed by Jesus of Nazareth in his incarnate self-revelation of God.

A basic presentation of Islam is reflected in the Five Pillars of Islam. Those Five Pillars are:

1. Frequent repetition of the creed, "There is no God but Allah; Muhammad is the messenger of Allah."
2. Pray five times daily, at dawn, mid-day, midafternoon, sunset and nightfall. Pray prostrate, facing Mecca if at all possible.
3. Almsgiving. Muslims are expected to share their possessions with the poor, with widows, and with orphans.
4. Fasting. Muslims have a month-long fast, Ramadan, during which they are required to abstain during daylight hours from eating, drinking, smoking and sexual relations. Muslims follow a lunar calendar, so the month varies from year to year in relation to the Western Gregorian calendar.
5. Pilgrimage. Every Muslim who can afford to is expected to make a pilgrimage to Mecca at least once in his or her lifetime. Their pilgrimage time in Mecca, and especially in the area near the Ka'Ba, is defined by rituals of devotion.[9]

Modern Islam has developed into sectarian branches (Sunni, Shi'ite, Sufi). Islam is practiced widely, almost universally, as one of the three primary monotheistic religions of the world.

[1] Lewis M. Hopfe and Mark R. Woodward, *Religions of the World* (Upper Saddle River NJ: Pearson/Prentice Hall, 2005), 242. John B. Noss, Man's Religions (New York: The Macmillan Company, 1956), 468. Cuthburt A. Simpson, "Introduction to Genesis," *The Interpreter's Bible*, 1 (1952): 440.

[2] Noss, Man's Religions, 469-472. Hopfe and Woodward, *Religions of the World*, 243-245.

[3] Francis I. Fesperman, *From Torah to Apocalypse* (New York: University Press of America, 1983), 63-70.

[4] David Graubart and Gertrude Wexler, "Synagogue," *Collier's Encyclopedia*, 22 (1987): 4.

[5] G. Ernest Wright, "The Faith of Israel, " *The Interpreter's Bible*, 1 (1952): 373-374. R. B. Y. Scott, "Exegesis of Isaiah," The Interpreter's Bible, 5 (1956): 231

[6] Lars P. Qualben, *A History of the Christian Church* (New York: Thomas Nelson and Sons, 1942), 29-30. Augustin C. Wand, "Dionysius (Denis)," *Collier's Encyclopedia*, 8 (1988): 238-39.

[7] Hopfe and Woodward, *Religions of the World*, 335-336. Noss, Man's Religions, 690-692.

[8] Hopfe and Woodward, *Religions of the World*, 339-340.

[9] Azed and Amina, *Islam Will Conquer All Other Religions and American Power Will Diminish*, 20-23. Hopfe and Woodward, *Religions of the World*, 344-347.

The Influence of Culture on Religion

Before beginning to focus on the development of Christian doctrines, consideration of the influence of human culture on the development of religious systems will help to round out the picture. I include this discussion with the clear understanding that some, if not all, of the ideas presented here will be unacceptable to some readers. I ask only that you give this information thoughtful consideration.

The Hebrew religion arose when Abraham came to believe that Chaldean moon-worship was an inadequate religion. He sensed that God was different and greater than that. He sensed a call to go out of that culture, away from that religion, and make a new start with God.

Abraham migrated as a nomadic herdsman around the Fertile Crescent to Canaan, where he believed that God was leading him. He and his clan lived there among the established inhabitants who were followers of a nature religion worshipping fertility deities called Baals. Religious understanding at that time was that the many deities being worshipped identified with specific portions of land over which they had control. The Hebrews came to believe that all of Canaan belonged to the God they worshipped, so Baal worshippers had no right to be living there. The Hebrew Scriptures record the battles and efforts at ethnic cleansing that resulted from these religious convictions.

Through the centuries, the Hebrew understanding of deity developed through polytheism to henotheism and finally to monotheism.

Along with the development of their belief in only one true God, the Hebrews also believed that they were God's chosen people and that God had an exclusive relationship with them. They believed all the non-Hebrew people could be related to their God (YaHWeH) only by becoming proselytes and entering into all the practices of the Hebrew sacrificial obedience to God.

Through the centuries of Hebrew national life, from the establishment of the kingdom under Saul until the destruction of the nation by the Assyrian and Babylonian empires, the most powerful figure in Hebrew civic and social life was the king. This cultural phenomenon led

> **Polytheism:**
> Belief in the existence of many deities.
>
> **Henotheism:**
> Belief in the existence of many deities but with one God superior to them all.
>
> **Monotheism:**
> Belief that there is only one God who is supreme and eternal and that all the other supposed deities are creations of human imagination.

the Hebrews to think of God as a divine monarch surrounded by a heavenly court of semi-divine beings (cherubim, seraphim and angels).

Before the time of the Babylonian captivity, the Hebrews also believed that good and evil in their lives came from God, the sovereign ruler of the universe who bestowed either his favor or disfavor on them. After the Babylonian captivity, Hebrew religion embraced moral dualism—the belief that good comes from God and evil comes through the temptation and influence of a demigod, Satan.

After the historical period of the Hebrew monarchy, the Hebrews lived under the dominance of other imperial powers (Babylon, Persia, Greece and Rome). Subservience to those non-Hebrew nations was a cause of bitter unhappiness to the Hebrews, who believed so deeply that they were God's chosen and exclusively favored people and that they were being prevented from living in splendid prosperity in their Promised Land.

This civic, political and military situation caused the Hebrews to look back with nostalgia and longing toward the "good old days," which for them was the reign of David. As time went on, a messianic hope arose among them that God would raise up a new "son of David" who would have the anointing of God upon him (messiah equals the anointed one) to enable him to raise a mighty army, be a divinely blessed leader, throw off the hated dominance of non-Hebrew armies, and restore the Hebrew nation to exalted blessing in the land of Canaan.

This was the kind of messiah the Jews longed for in the days of Jesus. This was the kind of king they believed God would one day raise up to deliver them. Everything that Jesus said or did that gave a hint of his supernatural nature and power stirred anticipations that maybe he was the long awaited deliverer whom God had at last raised up. There are numerous references in the Gospels that the crowds wanted "to make him a king," that there was a real possibility of a "messianic uprising" which would have brought harsh military reprisals by the Roman army. Jesus discouraged those feelings, trying to help the people understand that he had not come to be that kind of king. He said clearly to Pilate just before his death that "my kingdom is not of this world" (John 18:36). It seems evident that cultural situations had a significant influence on the origin and development of the messianic beliefs of Hebrew and Christian doctrines.

I am convinced that Jesus taught and exemplified a major refocus on the nature and character of God, which is significantly different from the beliefs and practices that developed among the Hebrews in the twenty centuries from Abraham to the time of the incarnation. Jesus called God "Father" (Abba) and emphasized the caring, outreaching, loving and giving character of God. We do not hear from Jesus any references to "kingly privileges" by God. There are no hints of "sovereign arrogance," which was so characteristic of ancient oriental princes. Jesus revealed a Father God who seeks to include as many people as are willing to be included, and he declared that his mission was to bring as many as possible into that fold. By his life and teachings, Jesus made important revelations about the character of God, the meaning of sin and salvation, the dynamics of alienation and reconciliation, and the "Paraclete principle" of God's presence and guidance. Those revelations make authentic Christianity unique among all the systems of religion in human history.

Religious Thought Before Jesus
— A Summary

Before we go into a study of the Christian religion specifically, it seems appropriate to summarize what we have found in our examination of the ages of human history before Jesus of Nazareth lived. This summary is a statement of my convictions.

The human species developed through the process of evolution as designed and controlled by God. Humans developed the capacity for rational thought, inquisitive searching, and aspiration for understanding. People observed that there were questions they could not answer and natural events they could not explain or control. This was the source from which came their sense of the existence of the supernatural.

As humans developed their awareness of the supernatural, they observed that certain natural phenomena influenced their lives in unexplainable ways. They came to attribute special powers to celestial objects (sun, moon, stars), natural objects (rivers, tides, wind), some animals (especially bulls because of their virility), and certain people (chieftains, witch doctors, shamans).

Thus there developed a sense that people in their daily lives are surrounded by and influenced by forces outside themselves and their own actions. Their human aspiration for well-being and prosperity caused them to want to find ways to relate to those forces and influences in ways that would gain favorable treatment and avoid unfavorable reaction.

The result was the rise of nature religions and animistic religions. The primary religious practices by which primitive people tried to influence the powers they worshipped were through the offering of sacrifices, typically animals and agricultural products burned on altars.

As time went on, their religious ideas and convictions were refined. People came to believe not that the moon was sacred but that a divine spirit resided in the moon; not that a carved idol was divine but that a divine spirit resided in the image. Out of ages of questioning and seeking, the religions of primitive peoples developed. The result was that many polytheistic and often tribal religions were being practiced by the time Abraham lived (about 2000 BC). The religious faith of the people was largely that each tribe had a relationship with a particular local deity that had chosen a place and a people to rule over.

During the last two millennia of pre-Christian history, some significant developments occurred in religious thought. Much of what most Christians know about those developments comes from our familiarity with the Hebrew religion.

Hebrew religion began when Abraham became aware of the inadequacy of Chaldean moon worship and sensed that a different deity was calling him to make a new start in a new place. Abraham's religion was basically a faith that God had chosen to establish a covenant relationship with him and his descendants in which God would be their exclusive God and they would be his chosen people.

Several centuries later, after the patriarchal period and the Egyptian residence era, Hebrew religion became more highly organized through ritual and sacrificial laws by the influence and leadership of Moses. The Hebrews had a personal name for their God (YaHWeH) that came from the desert experience of Moses in Sinai, but the nature of their faith was essentially a tribal religion centered on them as God's people and Canaan as God's land.

By the eighth century BC, however, polytheism was giving way to monotheism as a way of thinking about God. More emphasis on the moral requirements of religion emerged as some of the Hebrew prophets proclaimed the demands of justice in human relations, with more emphasis on upright character than on ritual performance.

As the period of the Hebrew monarchy ended with the Babylonian captivity and centuries of subservience to non-Hebrew cultures, two other prominent religious concepts became important in the Hebrew religious tradition.

The cultural and many faceted influences which came from living under dominance by hated adversaries gave rise to a yearning among the Hebrews for a deliverer (see pages 20, 28). The theocratic faith of the Hebrews that their king was divinely chosen and placed over them led to development of a messianic hope that God would raise up from the descendants of David, who had reigned in their "golden age," an anointed son of David (a messiah) who would throw off their oppressors and raise them to a new golden age of prominence and prosperity. This messianic hope became the basis of a triumphal Zionism—the belief that God would raise up a messiah to establish an earthly kingdom in Palestine and reign in Jerusalem. This belief is still very prominent in Hebrew religion and culture and lies at the center of the Christian premillennial understanding of eschatology.

A second significant development in Hebrew religion that coincided with the Babylonian/Persian period was a change in understanding of the nature of evil. Before the Babylonian captivity, the prevailing belief among the Hebrews was that problems in their lives were the result of God being displeased and withholding blessings or seeking to discipline and correct them by punishing their disobedience. I understand this to be moral monism (both good and evil coming from the same source). During the time that the Hebrew captives were in Babylon, they developed an understanding of evil that is moral dualism. Either from the influence of Zoroastrianism (see pages 14-15) or through the ongoing development of religious thought among the Hebrews, there developed the belief that good comes from God and evil comes from the influence of a demigod (Shaitin in Zoroastrianism and Satan, the fallen angel, in Judaism).

In summary, we can say that four primary characteristics of the Hebrew religion prevailed among the people at the time of the birth of Jesus.

1. They believed themselves to be uniquely and exclusively the covenant people of YaHWeH, whom they believed to be the only true God.
2. Their religious practices were the legal ritual and sacrificial systems originated by Moses and developed through the following centuries, becoming increasingly complex and burdensome as a result of interpretations by religious leaders through the generations. Micah's transforming understanding that rightness with God is a result of upright character rather than faithfulness in offering ritual sacrifices had become a feature in Judaism but had in no sense displaced the prominence of ritual and sacrificial practice.
3. The belief in moral dualism (God versus Satan) had become a firmly established feature of Hebrew religion.
4. The temple in Jerusalem was the center of priestly authority and the ritual and sacrificial practices of their religion, and the synagogues, scattered throughout the land, were centers for teaching the law of Moses and encouraging faithfulness to its precepts.

The Development of Some Theological Differences

In preparation for our examination of the development of Christian doctrine and the Christian church, I will explain some of the theological differences that affect what we believe about the development of sacred writings in Judaism and Christianity. The reader will recognize theological beliefs described here as the way many people still understand what they believe.

When we consider the historical development of religious thought and practice, we find fundamental differences in what people have believed through the centuries about how God has been active in the material universe, in human lives, and in the church. These differences in understanding and belief have significantly affected the way different branches of religion and church denominations and institutions have developed. The following explanations are arranged by historical sequence as much as possible.

About the Origin of the Material Universe

We begin with the foundational question of origins. Is the physical universe as we know it the result of direct creation or theistic evolution? While there is material evidence to be taken into account, the position a person chooses to take on this issue is ultimately a matter of faith and not scientific proof.

One question that has to be answered is whether the pre-Hebrew stories in the first eleven chapters of Genesis are historical narratives or inspired parables. I am personally persuaded that these marvelous stories are inspired parables, each of which has one central truth to teach about the origins and prehistoric development of human society in our relation to the eternal and Supreme God. This discussion will deal only with the creation stories in Genesis 1 and 2.

When trying to form one's faith about the origins of the physical universe, it is important to remember that scientific discussions on the subject deal with what has happened since the beginning. Science has nothing to say about what was before the origin of the material universe. Scientific studies can deal only with material evidence that reflects developments since the origin.

Before the rise of the theory of a "big bang" origin of the universe, the prevailing theory was that great streams of chemical elements flowed through space, and these streams of material atoms collided and spun off to form the stars and planets. When asked about the source of these streams of physical atoms, the common answer was, "We do not know."

It is equally true that discussions of the "big bang" theory also have to do with what happened since, and as a result of, that "big bang." The question of the source of all the energy of the universe compacted into what was there before the "bang" is scientifically unanswerable.

Whether the streams of atoms or compacted energy were naturally existing phenomena or whether the physical universe was the result of a "creation out of nothing previously existing" is not a question that can be answered by the "scientific method." What each of us believes about it is a matter of faith, and those of us who are Christians have no problem in dismissing the idea of a "no God natural universe" because we have accepted by faith that whatever exists, whenever and however it came into existence, is the handiwork of God.

I am personally persuaded that the concept of theistic evolution is most probably the way the universe developed. I find fewer problems with this idea than with a belief in a seven-day creation and organization of the universe and all living creatures. The biblical story in Genesis 1 describes a developmental process from the simple to the complex which I understand to be parallel to evolution and not contradictory. The biblical story declares forthrightly that the world, and everything in it, is the handiwork of God. Be sure of this: a supreme being who could make a world could make it at any time, in any way, and in any shape he chose. That, we who are Christians, can believe.

About the Nature of God

The earliest evidence of human awareness of the supernatural is related to the awe and apparent fear by primitive people of forces in nature they could not understand or control. From this there developed beliefs that natural objects like the sun, moon and stars had supernatural powers inherent within them.

Through the passage of time, human awareness developed into religions built upon the belief that natural objects (both heavenly and earthly), along with many different animals, were inhabited by supernatural spirits that were fashioned into deities by varied tribal groups. This was the prevailing situation in the areas of the Fertile Crescent (Persia to Egypt) in 2000 BC. Worship of heavenly bodies was predominant in Mesopotamia, the worship of fertility Baals was predominant among the Canaanite tribes, and the worship of Nile River and animal-headed gods was predominant in Egypt.

> **Polytheism:**
> Belief in the existence of many deities.
>
> **Henotheism:**
> Belief in the existence of many deities but with one God superior to them all.
>
> **Monotheism:**
> Belief that there is only one God who is supreme and eternal and that all the other supposed deities are creations of human imagination.

Beginning with Abraham and developing through the history of the Hebrew people until the time of the Babylonian captivity, the understanding of the nature of God continued to change. It began as a belief that their God (El) was one deity among many who was related to them alone and to the land of Canaan by his exclusive choice. Their belief in the nature of their God developed from polytheism to henotheism. Moses received the inspired revelation that God was not merely a generic Supreme God (El), but a Supreme Personal God (YaWeH, or I Am). By the eighth century BC, enlightened understanding was breaking through to great religious leaders like Isaiah that there is only one true God and that all other supposed deities are creations of human imagination.

A significant factor in the development of the Hebrews' understanding of the nature and character of God came from their cultural environment. During the kingdom period of the nation, from about the eleventh century BC until the end of their national period in the sixth century BC, the king was the most powerful person in the lives of the people. They believed the king was to be chosen by God and anointed by God and was the personal representative of God among God's people. Consequently, the idea developed that God was like the king at a divine level. Documents in the Hebrew Scriptures of the Old Testament reflect a description of God as an oriental monarch, giving favors if pleased, chastising and withholding favors if displeased, rewarding obedience, and punishing disobedience.

Observing the evolution of ideas about the supernatural across the span of 20,000 years helps us understand how religious beliefs and practices arose and developed. As humans tried to understand and relate to the material world around them, they came to the conviction that there were non-material powers that had influence and control over the material world in which they lived. A belief developed that an unseen spiritual world was the source from which the material world came into being, and which had ultimate control over the material world and their lives.

One difficulty for the ancient primitives was their lack of a frame of reference to help them understand the spiritual world. They had no language to describe a non-material world or the supernatural powers and God/gods that inhabit and control it. They had to reason out the ideas and develop language to express the concepts.

They lived in a material world, however, and their unanswered questions focused first on the world of physical nature around them.

- They observed the influence of the moon.

- They knew how much rain or drought, flooding river or barren desert affected their survival.
- A virile bull was essential to a herd.

They concluded, therefore, that there must be controlling spiritual powers inhabiting these natural objects and animals and others like them. It was only a short leap to conclude that supernatural powers would inhabit certain people. They came to believe in special powers of shamans, witch doctors, medicine men, priests, priestesses, tribal chieftains and theocratic kings (God chosen and enthroned).

An aside needs to be entered here. As the belief developed that special powers could be exerted by persons endowed by the supernatural, there developed the accompanying danger that these people would misuse any special capacities they had for selfish and manipulative purposes. And so it did indeed happen. Some used their special capacities for the benefit of others, but many used true or contrived capabilities to gain manipulative control over other persons, tribes and, later, realms for their own self-enhancement, wealth, power and prestige. The histories of primitive tribal cultures reveal this. It was equally true of later nation/state cultures. Read behind the lines in the Bible stories of the Hebrew kings from the Samuel/Saul beginning to the end of their national era in the Babylonian captivity, paying special attention to Solomon and Rehoboam. The blatant corruption of much of the Roman Catholic hierarchy in Europe during the Middle Ages is graphic evidence of this abusive misuse of assumed special endowment. And the phenomenon is current in the practices of numerous mass evangelists and supposed "miracle workers."

As people try to understand, relate to and describe the supernatural spiritual world, they use human, physical and natural world language and categories. As a result, varied concepts of supernatural and spiritual realities have developed through the centuries. We who are contemporary Christians meet this phenomenon when we read about physical descriptions of God (eyes of God, spoken words of God, hand of God, God walking on the clouds, etc.). We meet it as well in descriptions of life and the world beyond this world ("spiritual body" is an oxymoron; that is, the two parts of the expression contradict each other): streets of gold, mansions, crowns, lake of fire, etc. These expressions do not violate their purpose, for they are our human attempts to describe realities we have no adequate words for and to give expression to our concepts of highest and best, or lowest and worst.

This all reflects our finite inability to comprehend the ultimate realities of eternity. God is greater and more loving than our human minds can imagine, but thank God we can "touch the hem of the garment" because he has ever been seeking to reveal himself to the people of his creation, and he did so supremely and personally in Jesus.

About the Problem of Evil

Most religions that developed before the sixth century BC included a characteristic that I have described as "moral monism," a belief that both good and evil came as a result of the favor or disfavor of the deity under whose sovereignty the area and people existed. This belief belonged to the polytheistic stage of religious thought that many deities existed, that they competed with each other for dominion over geographic areas and tribes of people, and that they exercised control over the fate of "their people," bestowing favor for obedience and chastisement for disobedience.

As religious thought and belief developed toward monotheism from the tenth to the sixth centuries BC, a belief in "moral dualism" also developed. Good came from the favor of the sovereign deity, and evil resulted from the influence and action of a lesser semi-supernatural being, a demigod, a "fallen angel." This religious concept first developed among the Zoroastrians and the Hebrew exiles in Persia during the historical period before and during the Babylonian Exile of the sixth century BC. This belief in moral dualism and the role of a Satan demigod became an established feature of post-exilic Judaism and was carried over into Christian theology.

Later (see pages 94-96), as a discussion of Christian doctrine, I will present a different concept of the source of evil.

The Development of Sacred Writings in the Hebrew Religion

A Beginning Look at "Sacred" Writings

No one can deal seriously with many of the issues raised by the Hebrew and Christian religions without examining and making personal choices about how to understand the meaning of inspiration and the nature of the sacred writings of the two religions. Varied theories about inspiration have developed and been set forth in teaching and writing through the centuries of the Christian era. The theories rest on two basics:

- The role of God and the role of the writer.
- The way the two related to each other in the production of the documents that were later canonized as the sacred writings of the two religions.

Each of us needs to consider a beginning question: "Do I believe in a God who is infinitely present and actively involved in causing the universe to evolve through natural law and in helping people develop through rational searching and divine enlightenment into better informed and more morally responsible persons?"

It seems to me that these are undeniable characteristics of the infinite, moral and loving God that I believe the eternally Supreme Being to be. I believe our attempt to grasp the meaning of inspiration must be studied against the background of that kind of relationship between God and each of us.

As I study the Christian Bible, I understand the writers to describe themselves as having a sense that God was a present and guiding influence in their lives. The writers also reflect a personal awareness of what was going on around them in the world, about which they were applying rational understanding to the human concerns, moral values, cultural norms and religious influences that affected the circumstances in which they lived. Some of the writers reflect a sense that God had taken over their lives and minds and given them specific direction about what to say and do. Others, however, write as though they were describing and speaking to the prevailing circumstances, as God had given them insight to understand and act. The documents of the Bible reflect these differences in how the writers understood inspiration. The differences show up in the varied theories of inspiration still.

I am a theistic evolutionist who believes that God fashioned the material universe through the ages-long process of development from simple to complex. I believe that

God has guided the processes of religious thought and understanding through many phases that "in the fullness of time" came to fulfillment in incarnate revelation in the life and teachings of Jesus of Nazareth. I find in the Christian Bible evidence of limited human understanding of the nature and character of God counterbalanced by overwhelmingly wonderful evidence of God breaking through with revelations of himself, his compassionate care, and his gracious goals of fellowship and glory that we can share with him through trusting faith. I am a "Jesus theologian" who tries to test every religious concept I meet in Scripture or in human expression by the example of Jesus' life and teaching. I trust in the Holy Spirit to guide me in my faith in what I believe and how I live. This is how I approach Bible study.

I readily recognize that by traditional assessment what I have written above reflects what many Christians consider a "low view" of the Bible. I disagree. I consider it a "high view" of the Bible because my belief rests on a conviction that the documents that make up the Christian Bible came out of the dynamic activity of God working in the lives of the writers, compilers, editors and copyists, leading them to record accurately the state of religious thought and practice that prevailed at the time they lived. Serious study of the Bible reveals significant development in religious thought and practice during the twenty-five centuries from the migration of Abraham to Canaan until the canonizing of the New Testament (2000 BC to AD 400). Denying this gives rise to difficult problems in biblical understanding and interpretation. Human beliefs about the nature and character of God evolved and advanced a great deal from the time of Abraham to Moses, from Moses to the Babylonian captivity, and from the captivity to the birth of Jesus. The teachings and practices of Jesus put the imprint of incarnation on the nature and character of God. Jesus put an entirely new face on God and revealed a dynamically different meaning of religion for humanity. The difference between the Old Testament and the New Testament is far more than the difference between an "old covenant" and a "new covenant" (terms that mean very little to the average church member). The difference is as great and as significant as the difference between human thought and divine revelation.

So, is the Bible authoritative? Indeed, it has the very imprint of God upon it. The Bible is a trustworthy and authoritative record of God at work in his world and in his people. He led their development from primitive believers in nature religions to the time that the incarnation of the Eternal Son brought redemptive grace in reconciling reality as "salvation to all who believe."

The Hebrew Scriptures and the Old Testament Canon

The Sweep of History Covered

2100-2000 BC	Abraham migrated from Chaldea to Canaan.
1700-1600 BC	Hebrews went to Egypt under Jacob/Joseph with the clan.
1300-1200 BC	Hebrews left Egypt in the Exodus.
1050-1000 BC	Hebrew tribes were united into a kingdom by Samuel and Saul.
900 BC	Kingdom was divided under Jeroboam and Rehoboam into Israel and Judah.
722 BC	Northern Kingdom (Israel) was destroyed by Assyria and became the Ten Lost Tribes of Israel.
621 BC	Assyrian empire was conquered by Babylon.
586 BC	Southern Kingdom (Judah) was destroyed by Babylon and the Babylonian captivity began.
539 BC	Babylonian empire was conquered by Medo-Persia.
538 BC	Persian king Cyrus freed the Jews from captivity.
530-450 BC	Remnant groups of Jews returned to Jerusalem/Judea.

Background

- Hebrew religion was practiced and transmitted by oral tradition and individual writings for more than 1500 years before the first forms of a canon (established list of sacred writings) were recognized and accepted as authoritative.
- Through those centuries, religious authority and expression developed in the forms of cult rituals, chronicles of history, sacrificial laws, songs of religious experience, moral codes, prophetic proclamations and wise sayings. Gradually, more and more of these came to be recorded in written form, and eventually a body of authoritative documents (a canon) came to be accepted and established.
- Some Hebrew religious literature was put into written form as early as 900 BC; however, most of what we have in the Old Testament is from later times (600-200 BC).

Early References to Sacred Hebrew Writings

As early as the reign of Josiah (621 BC), there was a document recognized as "the book of the Law" that was found in the temple and became the authority for a period of religious reformation (II Kings 22-23). Internal references indicate that it was probably the nucleus of the book of Deuteronomy.

During the return from Babylon (450-400 BC), Ezra brought a copy of "the book of the law of Moses" (Ezra 7:6-10, Nehemiah 8-10). This is believed, by the internal provisions it contained, to be "P" portions of the Pentateuch ("P" meaning priestly code, referring to regulations of the sacrificial system of Jewish religion.) In some portions of the Pentateuch, God is referred to by the Hebrew name YaHWeH—the covenant name revealed to Moses at Mount Sinai. In some portions, God is referred to as El or Elohim—the generic word for God which meant The Supreme Being. The book of Deuteronomy is a restated summary with editorial revisions of parts of Exodus, Leviticus and Numbers. The dominant character of these varied portions of the Pentateuch has led to the widely held belief that the five books as we have them were put together by editorial work from earlier documents (J, E, P, D) in the period after the Babylonian captivity.

Before 200 BC, the Pentateuch had been translated into Greek. (Palestine was taken over by Alexander's armies in 332-331 BC. By that time, recognition of the Pentateuch as the primary scriptures of the Jewish religion was established.

The historical books (Joshua, Judges, Samuel and Kings) were put into writing, compiled and edited during the exile and afterward (550-100 BC). Compilation of the prophetic books and the "writings" took place largely following the exile. Some of them were not definitively accepted as scripture until after the beginning of the Christian era.

The "canon" of the Hebrew Scriptures (the Christian Old Testament) as we have it was established by AD 100, but variations of the Hebrew Scriptures continued in use by different groups of Jews.

Organization of the Documents in the Hebrew Scriptures

The Jewish scriptures are organized differently than the Christian Old Testament. There are three groupings:

The Law: Genesis, Exodus, Leviticus, Numbers, Deuteronomy.

The Prophets: The prophets are divided into two groups:
- Former prophets: Joshua, Judges, Samuel, Kings.
- Latter prophets: Isaiah, Jeremiah, Ezekiel, The Book of the Twelve.

Writings: Psalms, Proverbs, Job, Song of Solomon, Ruth, Lamentations, Ecclesiastes, Esther, Daniel, Ezra-Nehemiah, Chronicles.

The Protestant Old Testament is usually divided into four groupings:
Law: Genesis, Exodus, Leviticus, Numbers, Deuteronomy.
History: Joshua, Judges, I & II Samuel, I & II Kings, I & II Chronicles, Ezra, Nehemiah, Ruth, Esther.
Prophets: The prophets are divided into two groups:
- Major prophets: Isaiah, Jeremiah & Lamentations, Ezekiel, Daniel.
- Minor prophets: Hosea, Joel, Amos, Obadiah, Jonah, Micah, Nahum, Habakkuk, Zephaniah, Haggai, Zechariah, Malachi.

Poetic: Job, Psalms, Proverbs, Ecclesiastes, Song of Solomon.

A Brief Description of the Individual Documents[1]

> **J:** Sections that refer to God as YaHWeH.
>
> **E:** Sections that refer to God as El or Elohim.
>
> **P:** Sections that spell out the priestly requirements of the Mosaic Law.
>
> **D:** Sections that appear to be editorial additions to JEP materials in Deuteronomy.

Genesis

This is a book of beginnings. Included are eleven chapters of pre-Hebrew stories about beginnings. Hebrew history begins at Chapter 12 with Abraham. The records continue through the patriarchal period and the Egyptian epoch. The materials in this book were preserved and transmitted by oral tradition for many centuries. The book in its OT form was probably produced before 350 BC. When the component J, E, P and D documents were written is not known.

Exodus

This second book of the Pentateuch records the great events of the departure from Egypt and the Sinai period. During that time the masses of escaped slaves (loosely belonging to tribes by families) were organized. Civic, moral and religious structures for their common life were established. These documents clearly demonstrate the Hebrew conviction that the law as set forth by Moses was divinely revealed. All of these books of the Pentateuch probably share a common compilation of documents from long oral traditions.

Leviticus

Hebrew traditions were deeply religious. Central to their religious traditions were rituals and sacrifices that developed over the centuries of the patriarchal period and the Egyptian epoch. These were codified in the Mosaic Law as recorded in Leviticus. Civic, moral, dietary and religious regulations were included.

Numbers

This document records the story of the years after the departure from Sinai through the decades of the "wilderness wandering," the migration to Moab before the end of Moses' life, and the movement across the Jordan River into the land of Canaan.

Deuteronomy

The name of this last book of the Pentateuch means "second law." It is described in the text as Moses' last message to the Hebrews before his death. Its content is a review and expansion of the regulations as recorded from the Sinai period. This document is believed by many to be from a different compiler/editor than the other books of the Pentateuch.

Joshua

This book begins the group classified as "historical" in Christian literature. They are the "former prophets" in the Jewish organization. Joshua tells the story of the conquest (partial, never complete), division by tribal allotment, and settlement of the Hebrews in Canaan. The same evidences of J, E, P and D documents found in the books of the Pentateuch are also present in Joshua, so Joshua is often included with the other five books (referred to as the Hexateuch). It probably shares the same literary history of tradition and compilation as the books of the Pentateuch.

Judges

This book covers the historical period from 1200 to 1000 BC. It is made up primarily of stories about tribal leaders who were both civic and military leaders of the loosely connected and dispersed Hebrew tribes. During this period, the Hebrews shared the land with the Canaanite tribes who settled there before them. They did not intermingle or intermarry to any significant degree. There were periodic battles and raids on each other's crops. The "judges" we read about were primarily military heroes who led the Hebrews through those struggles. Like the Pentateuch and Joshua, this book was probably compiled in its present form after the period of the exile.

Ruth

This is an important story of the Moabite grandmother of David. It was surely written before 250 BC to resolve the question of how the Hebrews dealt with their ideal king having a non-Hebrew ancestor. David had a Hebrew grandfather, and according to this beautiful story he was "adopted" by his Hebrew step-grandmother Naomi.

I & II Samuel and I & II Kings

These four books (two in the Jewish scrolls) record the historical period from 1000 to 586 BC. These records cover the establishment of the loosely connected tribes into a kingdom under Samuel and Saul (demanded by the people for raising an army to protect against raids by nearby Canaanite tribes). The records extend through the growth and expansion of the kingdom during the reigns of David and Solomon, and through the division of the tribes into the Northern Kingdom (Israel) and the Southern Kingdom (Judah) in about 900 BC. The Northern Kingdom was destroyed by an Assyrian invasion in 722 BC; those tribes became the Ten Lost Tribes of Israel through intermarriage with Assyrians and Canaanites. The Southern Kingdom continued until it was destroyed by the Babylonians in 586 BC when Jerusalem, with its temple, was destroyed and the exile began for large numbers who were taken captive to Babylon. These records were most likely put into their present form during and after the exile but before 350 BC.

I & II Chronicles

These two books are included in the "historical" group in the Christian Old Testament but they are in the "Writings" group in the Jewish scriptures. The materials in Chronicles cover the same historical period as Samuel and Kings, with introductory genealogies from Adam to David. These materials are in the form of a historical drama that emphasizes the prominence of the Southern Kingdom and largely ignores the history of the Northern Kingdom. By comparison with Samuel and Kings, it appears that the compiler was less interested in historical accuracy and more concerned with the significance of the events as the compiler understood them. These documents are believed to have been put into present form from 350 to 250 BC.

Ezra/Nehemiah

These two books of the "historical" group in the Christian Old Testament are combined in one scroll in the Jewish scriptures and are included in the "Writings" group. The documents consist of stories about three people (Zerubbabel, Nehemiah and Ezra) who were leaders among the returning remnant that came back to

Jerusalem in groups from 520 to 450 BC. Zerubbabel and Nehemiah were builders who worked toward rebuilding the walls of Jerusalem and the temple. Ezra was a priest who worked to re-establish the sacrifices and regulations of the Mosaic Law among the returned group. These documents were most likely written after 450 BC and put into their present form before 250 BC.

Esther

This book may be best known for the fact that the word "God" does not appear in it. It is a group of stories about the conflict between Persians and Jews in Medo-Persian society after the Persian defeat of Babylon (539 BC). Remnant groups of Jews began to trickle back to Jerusalem, but many (probably most) of the Jews had become established in their lives in Babylonia/Persia. Some, like Mordecai and Esther, became influential, so harsh ethnic jealousies arose (Haman). The Jews avoided extermination and did a massive retribution. Chapter 9 tells of their celebration of Purim to mark that event. There is evidence that the Jews took an earlier harvest festival and renamed it for themselves for such a celebration. There is no historical verification in Persian records of a Queen Esther. She was most likely one of many "harem wives" of the Persian king and was elevated to "queen status" by the Hebrews for her role in their rescue from the designs of Haman. Internal dating by Persian kings indicates a time around 475 BC. The date of writing is not known, but is surely pre-Christian. The book appears in Christian collections of Jewish scriptures only after AD 100.

Job

This seems to be a literary work with no historical base, although it has been widely understood as historical. It is a collection of poems in the form of a debate dealing with the meaning of life and religion, with a central question about why innocent people suffer. Job has often been described as among the oldest of religious writings. General scholarly opinion, however, is that it was written after 500 BC using poetic oracles dating from before 900 BC. I disagree, believing it to be post-exilic. Before the exile, moral monism prevailed in religious thought. During and after the exile, moral dualism developed among Zoroastrians and Jews. This demigod of Zoroastrianism and post-exilic Judaism became the Satan of Christian theology. This developing dualism is the basis for the debate about the competition between God and Satan over the soul of

> **Moral monism** means that there is one divine being that reigns over a place and people and is the source of good (pleasure and blessing) and evil (displeasure and scourging).
> **Moral dualism** means that there is a supreme deity who is good and gives blessings if pleased, and a "one-step below supreme" demigod who is evil and creates evil in competition with the supreme deity.

Job, and the basis for the debate about the source and cause of evil in the poems of this book.

Psalms

This book is a collection of religious verse by numerous authors from varied periods of Hebrew history on a variety of subjects. In contrast to other Old Testament writings assembled of words from God to people and from people to people, the psalms are primarily words of people addressed to God. Many of the psalms were central to the worship life of the Hebrews. Indications are that they were compiled from 400 to 200 BC. By 100 BC the Psalms were included in the "Writings" section of the Jewish scriptures.

Proverbs

This book of "Writings" belongs to the literary genre called "wisdom literature." It includes collections of wise sayings from Solomon and others. Most of these sayings originated pre-exile but most likely were compiled in their present form after 400 BC.

Ecclesiastes

This "Writing" is also an example of "wisdom literature." Its identification with Solomon was traditional and largely uncertain. Its acceptance as scriptural was debated until the Synod of Jamnia (AD 90) decided in favor of including it in the Old Testament canon.

Song of Solomon

In Jewish scriptures this book is titled "Song of Songs," or "Canticle." This is the last of the "poetic books" of the Christian Old Testament. It is one of the "Writings" group of the Jewish scriptures. Like Ecclesiastes, it is traditionally associated with Solomon, also quite an uncertain association. Originally it was treated as folk poetry and sung as a wine song in banquet halls. By 700 BC it was being used in Passover liturgies.

Isaiah

Isaiah begins the "prophets" section of the Christian Old Testament and is the first of the "latter prophets" group in the Jewish scriptures. Isaiah is the first of four "major" prophets in the Christian Old Testament classification—major meaning lengthier, in contrast to the shorter "minor" prophets. In terms of importance, the eighth-century BC prophets Amos, Hosea and Micah were more influential in Hebrew history than Ezekiel and Daniel.

The Isaiah for whom the book is named was a prophet in the Southern Kingdom (Judah) before the Northern Kingdom (Israel) was destroyed by the Assyrians (722 BC). Chapters 1-39 focus on pre-Babylonian history (750 BC). Chapters 40-66 focus on the period of the exile and return to Jerusalem after the exile (600-450 BC). This major prophetic document, which begins with the oracles of the prophet and seems clearly to include the oracles of a second and probably a third later writer, was likely revised, altered and expanded until about 200 BC.

Jeremiah

This prophet lived during the last generation of the Southern Kingdom (Judah) before its end in the Babylonian Exile (625-570 BC). He was taken unwillingly to Egypt by Hebrews fleeing the Babylonian army just before the fall of Jerusalem (586 BC). It seems clear that later materials were added to his oracles before the document came to its present form.

Lamentations

This book follows Jeremiah in the Christian Old Testament because of its association with the prophet. It was titled "Dirges" in the BC versions of Jewish scriptures. In the AD Latin versions it was titled Lamentations of Jeremiah, as it still is in some Protestant versions. In the Jewish scriptures it is included in the "Writings" group, not the "Prophets" group.

The book is made up of five poetic dirges commemorating the destruction of Jerusalem by the Babylonian army in 586 BC.

Ezekiel

Ezekiel was a contemporary of Jeremiah in the last years before the beginning of the exile. Along with many of the Zadokite priests, Ezekiel was taken to Babylon. Many of his oracles declared that the Babylonian Exile was Yahweh's judgment on the corruption of the unfaithful nation. Like Isaiah, Ezekiel later turned to oracles of hope as he tried to encourage the Hebrews in captivity. He apparently died in Babylon about 570 BC. The book is likely a compilation by a later editor.

Daniel

This "major" prophet in the Christian Old Testament is one of the "writings" in Jewish scriptures. This document was likely written between 250 and 150 BC, during the Maccabean period (often called the inter-testamental period). The writer uses stories about Daniel and his friends during the Persian period (600-500 BC) and an apocalyptic vision attributed to Daniel. This document was most likely crafted to give encouragement to Jews who were suffering under the heavy hand of Antiochus Epiphanes (175-150 BC). The Seleucids were devotees of Greek culture and religion, which the Jews considered idolatry.

Hosea

This is the first of the last twelve books in the Christian Old Testament called the "minor" prophets because they are short, not because they are unimportant. In Jewish scriptures, the twelve are included in one scroll called The Book of the Twelve. It is a part of their "Latter Prophets" group.

Hosea was one of four great eighth century prophets (with Isaiah, Amos and Micah). He lived and preached about 750 BC in the Northern Kingdom (Israel). The book is an allegory (Hosea = God, Gomer = Israel, adultery = unfaithfulness and idolatry). This book provides the strongest Old Testament description of YaHWeh as a God of love and forgiveness.

Joel

Internal references indicate the document was written between 375 and 350 BC about a terrible locust plague as God's judgment on Jewish unfaithfulness.

Amos

This eighth century prophet lived around 750 BC in Tekoa, a town in Judah south of Jerusalem and Bethlehem. He was a shepherd and orchardman who traveled to sell his products at Bethel, a religious center just over the border in the Northern Kingdom. There he saw such immorality, corruption and injustice that he was moved to preach oracles of judgment and to call for righteous living. Social justice is the book's central theme (5:24).

Obadiah

Internal references indicate this document was written around 450 BC. The book is made up of oracles about Edom, the area southeast of Judah inhabited by the descendants of Ishmael and Esau. An alliance of nations had devastated Edom and Obadiah declared their suffering was God's judgment on them for their cruelty against the Jews.

Jonah

This book is a marvelous parable about God's care for all people—a very unwelcome idea to Jews. (This interpretation is disputed by those who believe the book to be historical experience.) In this parable, the main character, Jonah (patterned after an early eighth century preacher from Amittai) has an experience that illustrates the difficulty the Hebrews had coming to believe that God cared about the Assyrians in Nineveh just as he cared about them.

This is the most missionary book in the Old Testament. The author is not known. Internal evidences indicate it was surely written after the exile (400-200 BC).

Micah

Micah was a prophet in the Southern Kingdom (Judah). He lived in Moresheth, thirty miles southwest of Jerusalem on the road to Egypt. He was a contemporary of Amos (c. 750 BC), who lived twenty miles to the east in Tekoa. Apparently he was a small town craftsman. At that time, Judah was under threat as Assyria was driving south toward Syria and Israel—which Isaiah had told Ahaz would happen (Isaiah 7). Micah's primary concerns were low morality and unfair treatment of the poor (6:8). His understanding of the nature of religion (rituals or morality, or rituals and morality) was a major leap forward in religious thought (as I will develop later, see pages 96-97).

Nahum

This document is made up of poetic oracles gloating over the destruction of Assyria by the Babylonians, which occurred in 621 BC. The book presents God as vengeful and merciless toward enemies of the Hebrews and expresses the prophet's moral indignation against the cruel militarism in Assyria.

Habakkuk

This prophet grappled with some serious questions:
- Why does God permit evil?
- Does God use others (Assyrians, Chaldeans, Greeks) to punish people for their failings?

These oracles are believed to have originated in the 700s BC, with additions by copiers down to the 200s BC. The final conclusions written in the book are that faithfulness to God brings rewards in the end.

Zephaniah

This prophet wrote during the Assyrian period at the time of the destruction of the Northern Kingdom and the rise of Babylon (725-650 BC). His message was that the fate of the Northern Kingdom would also come to Judah. There is a word of hope, however, for while judgment would fall on evil nations, God would comfort Judah (his covenant people).

Haggai

The oracles of this prophet come from the Persian and "remnant return" periods (after 525 BC). He urged the returning exiles to rebuild the temple, but they were too busy growing crops for food and building walls for protection and houses to live in to be concerned about a temple. After all, most of these people had lived all their lives in Babylon without a temple. The oracles also reflect a developing animosity toward the Samaritans that was still very present in Jesus' day. The Samaritans were mixed race through intermarriage with Assyrians and Canaanites, and were thus believed to be unfaithful to their partial heritage as Hebrews and covenant people of Yahweh.

Zechariah

Zechariah was a contemporary of Haggai in the Persian and "remnant return" periods (after 525 BC). His call to the returning exiles was to rebuild the temple and restore the religious observances that were part of temple worship. Zechariah also reflects a developing messianic hope (a dream for a recovery of the golden age of David under a divinely anointed descendant of David). This document also reflects a developing moral dualism in the understanding of the nature of evil. This dualism arose along with, or as a result of, the influence of the Jewish exposure to Zoroastrianism in Babylon. The vision of Satan in Zechariah 3:1 is believed to be the first historical reference to Satan as the demigod source of evil by those who understand the book of Job to be a later theological drama grappling with the same problem of the nature of evil.

Malachi

This document is a part of a collection of anonymous oracles (along with Zechariah 9-14) which were originally a concluding appendix to The Book of the Twelve, when all of the minor prophets were compiled in a single scroll. The historical situation reflected in the oracles indicates a date of writing about 450 BC. The oracles raise the same questions as Habakkuk—why does God not rescue his people?—and conclude that God is waiting for their faithfulness before rewarding them with blessings. (Bring all the tithes ... and see if I will not open the windows of heaven.)

Observations

Take note of the numerous date references in the documents that are later than the period of the Babylonian Exile. I believe three factors are involved.

1. Across the 2,000 years involved, the art of writing advanced a great deal. In the earliest Hebrew history, writing was not a prominent part of nomadic Hebrew life. The people preserved genealogies and historical happenings by oral tradition, fathers helping sons memorize those traditions.
2. As time passed and writing became more a fact of life, written documents were created and some were preserved. The presence of obviously previous records in some of the documents of Hebrew Scriptures support this idea.
3. When the Babylonians destroyed Jerusalem and the temple and took many Hebrews into captivity, a major crisis came into their lives. The temple, with its Aaronic priesthood and Mosaic sacrifices, had defined the central focus of their religion. In Babylon, they were bereaved by their loss. While it cannot be definitely substantiated, I am persuaded that the synagogue was established as an institution to preserve their religious traditions. Whereas the temple had been a center for priestly activities and sacrifices, the synagogue was established as a place for preserving knowledge of the Torah and encouraging faithfulness to the Mosaic Law. The Babylonian captivity heightened the sense of need for written documents to preserve their traditions and to be used in the educational role of the synagogue.

These factors persuade me to agree with indications that many of the documents in the Hebrew Scriptures are indeed post-exilic in their current forms. Inspired authors and scribes produced documents from oral traditions and whatever earlier written passages were available to them.

These thirty-nine documents provide a chronicle of Hebrew/Jewish religious thought, faith and experience through the centuries from Abraham to the birth of Jesus. They were the sacred writings of the religion of Judaism that prevailed in first century Palestine. They were essentially embraced as sacred by the Christian movement and later carried forward as the Old Testament of the Christian Bible.

---

[1]These summaries are based on information gleaned from numerous standard texts and monographs. I have tried to reflect majority scholarly opinion, along with some positions uniquely my own.

A Group of Documents Called the Apocrypha

Apocrypha = Things Hidden
Also Called Intertestamental Writings[1]

The Sweep of History in the Apocrypha

- 332 BC Alexander the Great captured Jerusalem, died shortly thereafter, and the empire was broken up by competing generals of his armies.
- 320 BC General Ptolemy captured Egypt and Jerusalem. He made few changes from Alexander.
- 320 BC General Seleuceus captured Syria and northern areas.
- 198 BC The Syrian Seleucid, Antiochus the Great, took Jerusalem from Ptolemy. He treated the Jews well, and many Jews embraced Hellenic (Greek) culture and language.
- 175 BC Antiochus Ephiphanes succeeded his father. He was anti-Jewish, forbade Jewish religion practices, garrisoned Syrian troops in Jerusalem, set up a Zeus altar, and polluted the temple by sacrificing swine on the altar.
- 167 BC Hasmonean/Maccabeans under the leadership of Mattathias led Jews in a revolt against Epiphanes.
- 164 BC A guerrilla revolt led by Judas Maccabeus succeeded in liberating Jerusalem (except for a Seleucid fortress) and purifying the temple.
- 143 BC Simon Maccabeus (brother of Judas) captured the Seleucid fortress and destroyed it.
- 134 BC John Hyrcanus (son of Simon) extended Jewish rule in TransJordan and destroyed the Samaritan temple on Mt Gerizim.
- 63 BC A Roman legion under Pompey captured Jerusalem and made Judea a part of the Roman province of Syria.
- 37 BC Herod the Great and the Herodian dynasty replaced the Hasmoneans as the Roman vassals in Judea. This was the political situation in Judea when Jesus was born in 6/5 BC. Herod the Great died in 4 BC. His sons Antipas, Archelaus and Philip ruled over areas of Judea, Samaria, Galilee and Perea during the next generation.

The Traditional Documents of the Apocrypha

Tobit "God Is My Good"

Tobit was a poor, blind Jew in Nineveh (Assyria) who buried an executed fellow-Jew. His son Tobias served God faithfully, and to reward him the angel Raphael restored Tobit's sight.

Tobias married Sarah, moved from Nineveh to Ecbatana (Persia), and lived to an old age, faithfully serving God.

The document is primarily a folktale narrative about ordinary people who lived lives doing good and dreaming of a great new Jerusalem. It was most likely written after 250 BC in Palestine.

Judith

Judith was a wealthy Israelite widow who risked her life to slay the head of the Assyrian army. This is a folktale about a heroic woman (compare the story in Judges 4:17-22 about Jael, the wife of Heber, who killed Sisera, a Canaanite general, with a tentpeg). The story tells how Judith's brave deed broke the Assyrian threat and saved Jerusalem.

This story reflects practices found at other places in Maccabean Pharisaism. It includes Persian language and Greek features which generally indicate it was written during the Maccabean period.

The Rest of Esther

This is a group of short Greek additions to the text of Old Testament Esther. They include materials from and about Mordecai and Esther to fill out the text and correct some Jewish problems with the book (like Esther's marriage to a Gentile Persian king, of which there is no record in Persian history). These additions were written as late as 100 BC-AD 100, probably in Palestine and/or Alexandrian Egypt.

Wisdom of Solomon

This document is attributed to Solomon, although his name does not appear anywhere in the text. It reflects both Greek culture and language. Although its date is uncertain, it was probably written later than 100 BC. It includes many phrases from the Septuagint (a Greek translation of the Jewish scriptures made among the Diaspora [Dispersion Jews] in Alexandria).

Ecclesiasticus/The Wisdom of Sirach

Ben Sira describes himself as a scribe who recorded his insights of wisdom. This is the longest of the apocryphal documents. It is much like the Old Testament book of Proverbs. It was written by Ben Sira in Hebrew before 180 BC and translated by his son into Greek sometime after 132 BC. It was accepted as canonical by early Christians but was excluded from the Jewish scriptures after the Synod of Jamnia in AD 90 (which established the most widely accepted canon of Jewish scriptures) and by Protestants after the Reformation.

Baruch

It was written after 200 BC but set in the Babylonian Exile (after 586 BC). Jeremiah (Chapter 32) includes a Baruch, a friend of Jeremiah, who was taken to Egypt in the chaos just before the fall of Jerusalem. The text of Baruch shows kinship with Daniel 9, so tradition has Baruch also in Babylon. The text is divided into two parts—a corporate confession of sin, to be read with sacrifices in Jerusalem, and poems, one of praise to wisdom and one by the city of Jerusalem to the people of Jerusalem. The text has indications of four different writers and compilation by an editor. It includes different names for God and different religious concepts. It is believed to be encouragement for Jews of the Dispersion during Seleucid repression.

Letter of Jeremiah

This document presents itself as a letter by Jeremiah to Hebrews about to be taken into exile from Jerusalem to Babylon. In form, it is a sermon against idolatry and polytheism. Scholars date the document differently, but after 300 BC.

Greek Additions to Daniel

These were in the Greek manuscripts of Daniel but not in the older Hebrew text.
1. Prayer of Azariah: This document reports conditions of the Three Hebrew Children in the fiery furnace and includes their song as they danced in the flames. It fills out the briefer story in Daniel 3. The best estimate of when it was written is 200 to 150 BC.
2. Susanna: This is a story of a virtuous young woman falsely accused of immorality by two corrupt elders and cleared by the intercession of the wise young Daniel. It is a literary story about the triumph of virtue over villainy. It is estimated to be from the second century BC.

3. Bel and the Dragon. This is a story in three parts:
   - Daniel exposed the fraud of the priests of the Babylonian idol Bel;
   - Daniel proved the Dragon (a Babylonian mythical sea monster) was vulnerable to defeat;
   - Daniel survived a second, six-day time in the lions' den.

This is also estimated to be from the second century BC.

I Maccabees

This document tells of the beginning of the Hasmonean dynasty during a period of cultural flux. Greek and Semitic (Hebrew) cultures were co-mingled. The harshness of the Seleucids led to revolt. The document presents the Hasmonean/Maccabean revolution as the will of God, rising from the leadership of God.

It presents with reasonable accuracy the history of the region in that period. It was probably written after the death of John Hyrcanus in 104 BC.

II Maccabees

This document narrates the history of the period 180-160 BC. The first half is about the Seleucid oppression; the second half is about the victories of Judas Maccabeus. It presents it all as a divine plan of chastisement and deliverance.

This document includes theological ideas that are not in Jewish scriptures:
- Resurrection of the dead;
- Creation of the world out of nothing;
- Efficacy of praying for the dead.

It reflects a firm belief in the sanctity of the temple and all of the ritual details included in the Torah. It is estimated to have been written between 104 and 63 BC.

III Maccabees

This document is not Maccabean, so the title is a misnomer. It is about the struggle of Egyptian Jews under Ptolemy IV (221-203 BC), which is earlier than the Maccabean revolt period. It tells of Ptolemy attempting to enter the "holy of holies" in Jerusalem, being prevented by divine intervention, returning to Egypt determined to wreak vengeance on the Jews, and again being prevented by divine intervention. It was most likely written by Dispersion Jews in Alexandria sometime between a failed attempt to assassinate Ptolemy during the Battle of Raphia (a city in Palestine near Gaza) in 217 BC and the Roman destruction of Jerusalem in AD 70.

IV Maccabees

This document is in the form of a sermon about mastering the passions for religious reasons. Judaism is presented from the perspective of Stoic Greek philosophy, reflecting the developing influence of Gnosticism. This indicates the writing comes from the period 63 BC to AD 70.

I Esdras

This document narrates events in Judea from the Josiah reformation in 621 BC through the remnant groups returning from Babylon/Persia after the exile. It is thought that these may be Ezra's memoirs, which were put into writing not later than 100 BC. It includes some material from the Persian period that is not in the canonical Old Testament.

II Esdras

This is an apocalypse. It denounces the evils of the Roman Empire, deals with moral questions, and affirms God's justice, wisdom, power and goodness. The focus is on Jewish problems in the Roman period of the first century AD.

Prayer of Manasseh

Manasseh was one of the worst kings of Judah. He reigned from 687 to 643 BC. In this document he is presented as praying earnestly and humbly during the exile, being restored to the throne, and leading a reformation. This is referred to in II Chronicles 33:10-17 during a historical time when Babylon was rising in influence but before it crushed the Assyrian empire in 621 BC.

The main theological theme is the penitential restoration of evil persons. The writing is estimated in late first century BC.

Psalm 151 (only seven verses)

Not all ancient manuscripts have the exact 150 psalms of the Old Testament book. Some have psalms combined; some include this psalm. The Syrian Psalter has 151, 154 and 155. Codex Alexandrinus has 15 "odes" appended to the Greek Psalter after Psalm 151.

This document was written as a celebration (supposedly by David) of the way God blessed him and made him king.

Summary

This group of documents came from the last four centuries of the pre-Christian era. They have had a mixed history in both Jewish and Christian religions, being included as sacred writings at times and rejected at others. They have not been accepted as canonical scriptures by most of Protestant Christianity. Nevertheless, they are valuable for what they record of the history, struggles and religious faith of the Jewish people who lived under Greek, Egyptian, Maccabean and Roman influences.

[1] Extensive articles about the Apocrypha are found in: Robert F. Pfeiffer, "The Literature and Religion of the Apocrypha," *The Interpreter's Bible*, 1 (1952): 391-419; and *The New Oxford Annotated Bible* (1991): APiii-AP 364.

Earliest Christian Developments

Before we consider the development of the sacred writings of the Christian religion, it is important to focus on the earliest developments among the followers of Jesus. The sacred writings came out of those early developments and the expansion that resulted from them.

When Jesus was crucified, everything changed for his followers. The Gospels record that Jesus told them clearly that he would be killed and would arise from death, but they were neither able to grasp what he was saying nor understand what it meant.

There is a truly fundamental difference between people saying what they believe about God and what God has revealed to them on the one hand, and what God did when Jesus lived and taught. I am convinced that Jesus was not merely talking about God but was in fact God revealing himself in an incarnate personal connection. My study of the development of religious thought within humanity has persuaded me that God's unique self-revelation made in the life of Jesus is the most significant event in the history of religion in all of humankind. If you want to know about God, look to Jesus, his life and his teachings.

The Disciples' First Experiences

After Jesus was executed and was no longer physically present with them, his small group of followers had to come to grips with what it all meant. After all, what Jesus had said and done was very different from the religion they had been taught and experienced up to that point.

They had been, like others of their generation, immersed in the messianic hope of Judaism. Even after they had shared time with Jesus, seen him live, heard him teach, gone through the events of his death, and experienced his resurrection, they still really understood very little. In the record of the ascension event in Acts 1:6ff they asked him, "Lord, will you at this time restore the kingdom to Israel?" That was Jewish messianic hope. It seems clear that the truth Jesus spoke to Pilate, "My kingdom is not of this world" (John 18:36), had not yet become real to them.

Those earliest disciples of Jesus had to decide for themselves what they really believed about Jesus and what that meant for them. What were they supposed to do now that Jesus was physically gone? And they had to choose whether they were willing to do it. I believe the event recorded in John 21:1-19 reflects their efforts to find their way. When Peter said, "I'm going fishing," and six others said, "We will go with you," they appeared to be asking themselves, "What do we do now? Do we go back to the way we lived before we began going about following Jesus?"

On the shore of Galilee that morning, Jesus answered the question for them. He challenged Peter's faith and devotion and said to him, "Follow me." Faith in Jesus meant a changed life for them. Henceforth, they were to be living witnesses, by example and by sharing their faith, of what Jesus had revealed about God and the relationship they now had with him.

Fundamental Truths Jesus Left with Them

As a result of their experiences with Jesus and through the work of the Holy Spirit in their lives, some great fundamental truths became real, life-changing and life-motivating to those first Christians.

First, Jesus had revealed something wonderfully new about the character of God. God is not like a self-centered, capricious monarch who metes out favors or chastisement on a personal whim. God is like a loving father who cares so much for us that he cannot make himself abandon us to our own hopeless moral and spiritual ruin. Jesus revealed that God wants nothing more than to forgive our chosen destructive values and reconcile us to him through a new beginning of faith and trust and transformed lives.

As the followers of Jesus gave witness of their faith in him as the Messiah and proclaimed the good news about Jesus that they had come to believe, the Jewish leaders became less and less tolerant of them. Increasingly, the disciples were driven out of the temple and the synagogues. Through their ongoing experiences, a second truth became clear to them—that Jewish exclusiveness did not have any standing with God. Simon Peter learned it at Joppa and Caesarea (Acts 10), and Paul learned it on his first missionary journey (Acts 13-14). The open inclusion of all people in the embrace of God became the established faith among Christians (Acts 15).

A third great truth came to his followers when Jesus left them with a commission. As the Hebrew religion developed, the Jews gladly embraced belief in the covenant with Abraham (Genesis 12) that their God would bless them and make them prosperous. They believed, however, that they were an exclusive, chosen people. So through their history they conveniently forgot the part of the covenant where Abraham and his descendants were to be a channel through which God's blessings flowed to all the people of the world. Jesus changed that by leaving his followers with this truth: every disciple (a person who learns from Jesus and seeks to follow him) is also to be an apostle (a person who is sent on a mission to spread the Gospel). To a sad and significant degree, Christians have treated the commission from Jesus like the Hebrews treated the covenant with Abraham, grasping on to the part that seems personally favorable and bypassing the part that applies to others. In large measure in Christian history, the spread of the Gospel has been made the work of the "ordained" few instead of the "commissioned" many.

The Beginning of Church Life

The development of Christian churches began during the first generation following the years of Jesus' physical life. Groups of Christians in local areas became established by spending time together for fellowship and encouragement. They had no legal standing as a religious group with the occupying Romans, who considered them a rogue sect of Judaism. Most of them belonged to what we would call the working class, so they typically gathered in the evenings. They met in the home of a member of the group and usually shared a meal. Thus developed the "house churches" referred to in the New Testament.

Those first Christian churches had little in the way of institutional organization. Their first officers included an overseer (bishop) who was something like a convener of their gatherings. They had elders who were respected for their experience, knowledge and wisdom, and deacons who attended to the daily needs of dependent members of the group.

They gave themselves a name, "*ecclesia*" (a compound Greek word meaning "a called out group." The name was adopted from the Popular Assembly of citizens in the Greek city state of Athens in the early sixth century BC.)[1] The choice of names was intended to indicate that they thought of themselves as people who had heard a message from God to be "a called out people," a band of disciples of Jesus. As such, they had a central feature that they called "*koinonia*" (variously translated as fellowship, communion, partnership). The basic meaning is "shared in common," and it was used by the early Christians to describe what they shared in common—their mutual commitment to Jesus as Lord and their resulting relationship of trust in God.

The Pentecost Event and Its Significance

Another vital and transforming part of early Christian experience was the Pentecost event. Before his death, Jesus had promised that when he was no longer physically present, the Holy Spirit would come to be the living presence of God with them. The Christians experienced the Holy Spirit's dynamic presence among them in the Pentecost event.

This development was a continuation and culmination of a great thread of truth about God, reaching back in human history and experience, as the Emmanuel/Paraclete expression of God's love and care.

About 730 BC, the Assyrian Empire was expanding from the northeast and the nations of Syria and Israel were threatening to invade the kingdom of Judah. Ahaz, king of Judah, feared his adversaries and tried to get Egypt to support him. The prophet Isaiah urged Ahaz to trust in God instead of in military alliances. Ahaz scoffed at Isaiah's urging, so Isaiah told him that he would be given a sign that God had not forsaken Judah. Isaiah told Ahaz that a boy would be born and named Emmanuel (God is with us). Before the boy was old enough to refuse evil and choose good, the two adversary kings would be eliminated, but every time the boys played in the street and called to their playmate, "Emmanuel, Emmanuel," the king would be reminded that, even in a time of national crisis, God is with his people and has not abandoned them. (Read about this historical event in Isaiah 7.)

When Matthew was inspired to write the Gospel that bears his name, he recorded the great tradition that the name Jesus (which means YaHWeH is salvation) had been revealed to Joseph before the babe was born because he would be a savior/deliverer of his people. Matthew added the declaration that the birth of Jesus was in the great Emmanuel tradition of Isaiah. As God was with his people in times of national crisis (as with Judah), God is with his people who are sinful to save them from their sins. (God cares enough for us that he cannot bring himself to abandon us to the utter ruin of our sinfulness.)

The Emmanuel/Paraclete thread of revelation and promise is reflected in some words of Jesus to his disciples on the evening before his death. In John 14:16 it is recorded that Jesus promised, "I will pray the Father, and he will give you another Paraclete, to be with you forever even the Spirit of truth." In John 14:26 it is recorded that Jesus identified the promised Paraclete as the Holy Spirit.

Some basic Greek word study will expand and enrich the meaning of this wonderful passage. The word *Paraclete* is a compound word meaning "to call alongside to aid." I am convinced by the context that Jesus meant not that he would respond to our call and come to our aid, but that God loves us so much that he is drawn by his love to us and cannot let himself abandon us.

While Jesus told the disciples that he was going away, he promised that he would not leave them abandoned or orphaned (John 14:18).

When Jesus promised that the Father would send them *another Paraclete*, he used the word *allon*, which means "another of the *same* kind," instead of the word *eteros*, which means "another of a *different* kind."[2] This distinction gives credence to Jesus' promise that, "As I have been God present with you in caring love to aid and guide you," now that I will no longer be with you in physical presence, "the Holy Spirit will be God abiding with you in loving and helping presence."

In the passage in John 14, Jesus further told the disciples that the new Paraclete that the Father would send could not be "received" by the world because it could neither "see" nor "know" him (verse 17). The word translated "receive" is from the

Greek word *lambano*, which means "to take hold of." The word was indeed used to mean "receive," but "to take hold of" could just as correctly mean "to seize." The context leads me to conclude that Jesus was promising that the world in its enmity would not be able to seize and thwart the ministry of the Holy Spirit, as it was about to do to him in the arrest and crucifixion.

As Jesus' disciples were facing the imminent trauma of his violent death, his marvelous promises laid the foundation for their understanding of Pentecost. The Emmanuel (God is with us) thread that began with Isaiah (The Great God of Israel is with Judah in her national crisis) and found wonderful meaning in the birth of Jesus (God the Eternal Son is with sinners to save them from their sins) would now become to the Christians *another Paraclete of the same kind as Jesus* (God the Holy Spirit ever-abiding in love and grace to guide, empower and bless). What a marvelous revelation and promise of love and blessing!

A First Generation Summary

This, then, is what happened in the first generation of the Christian movement after the years of Jesus' incarnate life. As the first Christians, the disciples had to decide what they believed about Jesus, and what it meant in their lives now that he was no longer physically present. The sharp differences between the Christians and the traditional Jews led to the Christians being driven out of the temple and synagogues. Pentecost occurred and the Christians experienced the Holy Spirit as the new Emmanuel (God is with us, drawn to our side by divine love and desire to reconcile). As Jesus had revealed the true character of God in his incarnate living, the Paraclete of the "same kind" remained to bring salvation (reconciliation) to alienated sinners.

The vast difference between Judaism and Christianity led the Christians to separate from former Jewish religious practices. Christians gathered in groups for fellowship and support, and local churches came into being. During the first generation, the opposition of the Jewish leaders in Jerusalem led to the scattering of Christians and the beginning of churches in several cities in Palestine. Through earlier centuries, Jews had been scattered to cities around the eastern Mediterranean basin by trade and by the Greek and Roman dominance over Palestine. Travel among the Jews of the Diaspora (Dispersion) led to churches being founded in some of the cities where there were groups of Jews. The early Christians' growing awareness that Jewish exclusiveness was not in God's plan, along with the commission by Jesus, led to the next development. During the second generation of the Christian era, Christianity became a missionary religion and a largely Gentile religious movement.

Around AD 45, the conversion of Saul, a Jew from Tarsus, and a rising missionary spirit in a church in Antioch of Syria led to the beginning of Christian missions. Saul (later Paul) and Barnabas were sent out to take the Christian Gospel to the world beyond Palestine. They went northwest toward Europe instead of southwest toward Africa (we can readily believe this happened by leadership of the Holy Spirit), and this definitively influenced the developing history of Christianity.

During the historical period of the missionary activity of Paul (AD 45-65), churches were established in many cities of Asia Minor (modern Turkey) and the peninsula of Greece. At the same time, written records began to be produced. Paul's letters to various churches described the Christian movement and set forth the growing definition of what Christians believed and how they lived. An ever larger body of written documents was recorded through the next half-century. It was from among a great multitude of such writings that the Christian churches in the second and third centuries AD gathered and studied and sorted and finally agreed that twenty-seven of them had enough evidence and character of Holy Spirit inspiration to be declared sacred. These documents the Christian movement canonized, and they became the books of the New Testament.

[1] Lars P. Qualben, *A History of the Christian Church* (New York: Thomas Nelson and Sons, 1951), 1-2. "Ecclesia," *Encyclopedia Britannica*, Internet search January 7, 2015.

[2] G. Abbott-Smith, *A Manual Greek Lexicon of the New Testament*, (Edinburgh: T. & T. Clark, 1950), 22.

How We Got the Christian Bible

The Meaning of "Canon"

The word "canon" is used to describe the thirty-nine documents included in the Old Testament and the twenty-seven documents included in the New Testament of the Christian Bible. There are also fourteen (seventeen) documents called the Old Testament Apocrypha (see pages 55-60). When the leaders of the Christian movement set about to establish a canon of sacred writings, they embraced the accepted Hebrew writings as sacred and included them as the Old Testament (see pages 41-54). Some collections of "canonized documents" also included the Apocrypha, sometimes called "Intertestamental Books." After the Protestant Reformation, most editions used by Protestants omitted the Apocrypha.

The following discussion considers the documents of the New Testament group because they are of primary interest to us as Christians.

The word "canon" came from a Greek word meaning "a measuring rod." The word was first used to designate the approved list of sacred Christian writings by Origen, bishop of Caesarea, in about AD 250. It established a standard for evaluating documents to determine whether they were of apostolic authorship and/or inspired by the Holy Spirit. The historical development of the canon came through the sifting and sorting by the churches and their leaders as they evaluated writings to select those appropriate for use in Christian worship and for authoritative Christian teaching.

Our Approach in This Section

This discussion does not attempt to deal with matters of theology or the comparative value of the various documents. Our focus is the historical process through which these 27 documents came to be written and how they came to be this enormously influential group of writings called the New Testament.

A vital part of any discussion of Christian sacred writings is the question of how we understand inspiration (see pages 41-42).

Lest there be any question about what I believe, let me affirm this now. I am absolutely convinced that:
- The eternal God is the source of all of the material universe and of human life.

- He has been actively involved in the history of the universe and of humanity at every point and in all time.
- He actively related to the people who wrote and compiled the New Testament, inspiring them in their search to understand him and his will for humanity, and inspiring them to write and preserve the documents in the New Testament.

The Christian New Testament is indeed a wonderfully mysterious and inspiring divine/human collection of documents.

Historical Origins

Jesus of Nazareth was born 6/5 BC and died about AD 26. The Hebrew Scriptures were the sacred writings for the Jewish people of that generation, and the early Christians continued to use them in worship. The life and teachings of Jesus were what I believe to be the Christian Gospel, the incarnate revelation of the love and grace of the supreme eternal God. The things Jesus did and said and taught were retained in memory and transmitted by oral teaching and preaching for many years. Over time, written records were produced and collected.

The Apostle Paul became an itinerant preacher during the years AD 46/7 until AD 65-69. He led the establishment of churches in central Turkey, along the Aegean coast of Greece, and in the southwestern quadrant of Turkey, and maintained contact with them through subsequent visits and letters. His letters were the earliest writings that later became documents included in the New Testament.

Through the preaching and witnessing of the apostles and other Christians, churches were also developing in places like Jerusalem, Antioch in Syria, Alexandria in Egypt, and Ephesus in Asia Minor, along with a Christian community in Rome. The Jewish Dispersion (Diaspora) and widespread travel in the Roman Empire had created a fertile environment for the spread of Christianity.

As the generation of eye-witness disciples was dying off, the chaos of the Romans' destruction of Jerusalem (AD 70) was dominant in the eastern Mediterranean world. Four Christians were moved with inspiration to create written records of the life and teachings of Jesus, which became the four Gospels. Some general tracts and various kinds of documents that other Christians were writing became accepted by the churches and are included in the New Testament. Far more writings were not believed to be apostolic or inspired and therefore were not deemed to be authoritative for use in worship and for guidance in life; they consequently were not included in the New Testament.

The Sequence of the Production of the New Testament Documents

I Thessalonians (AD 51-52)

On his second preaching mission, Paul went into Greece and led the formation of churches in Philippi, Berea and Thessalonica. After he moved on to Athens and Corinth, he heard that the Christians from Thessalonica were troubled and uncertain about the Christian hope for end times and by accusations made by non-Christian Jews against Paul. He wrote this earliest letter from Corinth to encourage and instruct them.

II Thessalonians (AD 52)

It appears that some of the Thessalonians misunderstood Paul's letter. This second letter seems to have been written shortly afterward to further explain his teaching about the Christian hope concerning the end of time. Note that in Paul's early letters he wrote as though he expected Christ to return in the generation in which they were living.

Galatians (AD 54-55)

On his third preaching journey, Paul visited churches in central Turkey (Galatia) and then moved on to Ephesus, as he had promised earlier. He worked there for more than two years, establishing churches in cities in the region. (These cities correspond to the seven churches named in Revelation 2-3.) During that period Paul wrote to the Galatians to address whether Gentiles had to become Jewish proselytes and fulfill Jewish ritual requirements before they could become Christians. Paul's answer was a firm and final "no;" the grace of God is open to all.

I Corinthians (AD 54-56)

While Paul was preaching in the Ephesus area, he received a letter questioning the conduct of some Corinthian Christians (I:7:1, I:8:1, I:12:1). Paul wrote this first letter in reply, answering the questions and including at length some pastoral instructions and admonitions.

Apparently, something happened that caused strained relations between Paul and the Corinthian church. He left Ephesus long enough to go to Corinth for a short visit. There was a painful confrontation (referred to in II:2:1) with some Corinthians who had become adversaries of Paul's preaching and leadership. There is no other reference to such a visit; however, there is some evidence that he wrote another letter about that situation, fragments of which some people believe are contained in what we have as II Corinthians.

II Corinthians (AD 57-58)

Paul left Ephesus with the intention of visiting the churches in Greece. He went from northern Greece to Philippi. While he was in Macedonia he received word that things had cleared up in Corinth, and now there was harmony between him and that church. He wrote this letter to express his joy that things were resolved and to continue his pastoral instruction and encouragement to them.

Romans (AD 58-59)

Paul went down through Macedonia and Greece to Corinth on his way to Jerusalem to deliver the benevolent offering he had collected from the churches on his third journey. From Jerusalem, Paul was determined to begin another mission farther west, to Rome first and then on to Spain. While he was at Corinth, Paul wrote Romans and sent it on ahead to identify himself to the Christians in Rome and to serve as a prelude to his planned coming. This document has been acclaimed through the centuries as the most complete theological writing in the New Testament.

When Paul arrived in Jerusalem, he was placed under protective custody to prevent angry Jews from killing him. Political machinations forced him to appeal to the emperor (a privilege he had as a Roman citizen). This resulted in two years of imprisonment in Caesarea and then on to Rome. The book of Acts ends after the two years of imprisonment in Rome. The outcome of his appeal to Caesar is not known. There is an ancient tradition that he was kept in prison there until he was beheaded during the Neronian persecution of Christians in Rome in AD 65. Some people believe he was released, made his mission to Spain, wrote some later letters, and was again imprisoned and martyred in AD 70. There is no definitive historical evidence of this tradition.

Internal evidence indicates that, while imprisoned in Rome, Paul wrote four letters that are included in the New Testament.

Philippians (AD 63-65)

The fellowship between Paul and the Philippian church was evidently the most cordial and least contentious of any of the churches. In the letter, Paul writes about his joy in that fellowship and of his gratitude for the gifts of support the Philippians had provided for his work and during his imprisonment.

Ephesians (AD 63-65)

Some early manuscripts of this document, and some early writers who refer to it, do not include an address to Ephesus. The content is more like a Christian tract than a letter because it does not deal with an individual church situation. It is widely believed that this was intended to be a circular letter that would be shared and read in the churches in the area around Ephesus. This practice of circulating letters is referred to in Colossians 4:16. Ephesians is one of the last of Paul's surviving letters (along with Colossians) and, while we are not studying content in this series, it is my conviction that these two letters preserve for us the distilled essence of Paul's most mature and developed understanding of the Christian faith and life.

Colossians (AD 63-65)

This letter, very similar to Ephesians, is almost like a brief summary sent along to be circulated with personal greetings.

Philemon (AD 63-65)

This is a brief personal letter, written by Paul to an individual, Philemon from Colossae, who had a church meeting in his house there. One of Philemon's slaves, Onesimus, ran away and came to where Paul was. Onesimus became a Christian through Paul's witness. Paul sent Onesimus back to make things right with Philemon and to appeal for Philemon's pardon. Opinions differ over when this occurred and where Paul was: some think Ephesus in AD 54-56, some think prison in Caesarea in AD 59-60, and some think prison in Rome in AD 63-65. Based on the people included in the personal greetings in verse 23 (compare Colossians 4:10-15), I am inclined to believe it was during the Roman imprisonment.

These ten documents are almost universally believed to be authentically Pauline. (Ephesians and Colossians have been the most questioned.) There are other documents included in the General Epistles which are attributed by some to Paul but are widely believed to be non-Pauline. We will discuss them later as a group.

We turn now to the four Gospels. We begin with some background material: Matthew, Mark and Luke are called the Synoptic (with one view) Gospels because they present similar approaches

---

In the Synoptic Gospels, there are four identifiable bodies of material:

1- The **Gospel of Mark**, most of which is also in Matthew and Luke.

2- **Q**, which is material found in Matthew and Luke but not included in Mark.

3- **M**, which is material in Matthew but not in any of the other Gospels.

4- **L**, which is material in Luke but not in any of the other Gospels.

to recording the life and teachings of Jesus. The fourth Gospel, John, is quite different in the material included and the interpretations made by the writer and contains a lot of material not included in the Synoptic Gospels.

Mark (before AD 65)

Mark is almost universally agreed to be the first of the Gospels written. It is the simplest narrative record of what Jesus said and did of any of the Gospels. Almost all of Mark is included in Matthew and Luke, much of it word for word, leading to the idea that Matthew and Luke had copies of Mark that they used as they compiled their documents. Mark is believed by tradition to be recorded from Peter's account while in prison in Rome before his martyrdom in Nero's persecution. The compiling of this first Gospel is dated before AD 65. It is believed to have been written for Gentile readers in Rome.

Matthew (AD 75-90)

This document includes material from Mark, Q and M. Its primary focus is on Jesus as Messiah fulfilling the Jewish messianic hope. It seems probable, therefore, that it was written in Jerusalem (Palestine) for Jewish Christian readers.

Luke (generally dated AD 75-90, but I believe before AD 65)

This document includes material from Mark, Q and L. It has a more universal focus, with stories about Jesus' concern for the poor and his acceptance of non-Jews (e.g., the Good Samaritan). Written for Gentile readers, it is believed to be by Luke, the physician companion of Paul on his second and third missionary journeys. The writer of this Gospel declares he did careful research before writing and identifies Acts as a follow-up document.

Acts (generally dated AD 80-90, but I believe before AD 65)

This is the second volume of the Luke/Acts documents Luke wrote for Theophilus. Acts is the only organized record of the early church development included in the New Testament. It includes accounts of events following the resurrection and the ascension, and following Pentecost. It records Paul's missionary work and the transition of Christianity from a group of Jewish converts in Palestine to a mainly Gentile movement westward around the Mediterranean Sea. Acts ends with Paul in Rome under house arrest; apparently Luke did not know the outcome of

Paul's appeal to the emperor or he would surely have included it. Thus I conclude that Luke and Acts must have been written before Paul's death in AD 65-70.

John (AD 90-100)

Tradition holds that the Apostle John wrote the fourth Gospel from Ephesus sometime after AD 75. (Many interpreters believe it was written by a John the Elder rather than the apostle, which influences whether it is believed that the John in exile on Patmos of Revelation 1:9 was the apostle or the elder.) This Gospel differs from the Synoptics both in the amount of material unique to it and in the writer's emphasis on interpreting the meaning of the events and teachings of Jesus by focusing on the "signs" that reflect who Jesus was and what his mission was.

I & II Timothy and Titus

The New Testament includes these three letters called the Pastorals. Throughout much of history they were thought to have been written by Paul to two young preachers. However, in recent decades they have been widely considered to be the work of a disciple of Paul who wrote after his death, probably even after AD 100. Two streams of content information affect this difference. The language and style in the Pastorals differs from the letters that are certainly Pauline, and the degree of church organization in the Pastorals seems developed beyond that during Paul's life. Those who believe the Pastorals are Pauline generally believe that Paul was released from the Roman imprisonment of Acts, that he had additional unrecorded years of missionary activity, that he was later imprisoned again, during which time he wrote these letters, and that he was martyred in the AD 70 chaos instead of the AD 65 Neronian persecutions.

The New Testament also includes eight documents called General Epistles. These are generally dated from AD 60-100+; they come from a variety of sources; they treat varied subjects; and they fared differently in the process of acceptance into the approved canon.

Hebrews (before AD 70)

Hebrews is not so much a letter as it is a treatise on Jesus as the fulfillment of the high priest's role and the messianic hope of the Jewish nation. The text has no name included and the authorship has long been debated. It was a long while before Hebrews was accepted into the canon.

James (after AD 65)

James was a common name in the first century, so there is no definitive way to identify the author. He evidently was familiar with Paul's preaching, for he clearly seems to write a different message in the works/faith passage (2:14-26), and his "response" approach in 1:12-16 seems different than Paul's "election" emphasis in Romans 8 and 9. It seems certain that he wrote later than Paul.

I Peter (AD 60-64)

This letter has been widely accepted as apostolic, from Peter in Rome before his martyrdom in AD 63-64. It has been noted by some, however, that it is addressed (1:1-2) to Jews of the Dispersion in Asia Minor, where Paul worked extensively but where there is no record that Peter worked, and that it was transcribed by Silvanus (Silas) (5:12), who was a working associate of Paul. It was among the earliest approved documents by churches.

II Peter (AD 90-110)

This document was early believed to be pseudonymous (written by someone using Peter's name to try to gain it more acceptance). It was late in the canonizing process before it was approved and was among the last works to be included in the canon.

I John (after AD 90)

This document is a tract, not a letter. It is believed to be by the same author as II and III John, who identifies himself as an elder. Many believe he was from the Ephesus area and is the author of the Gospel of John and of Revelation. First John was widely recognized as apostolic and was early included in the accepted documents by the churches.

> Authorship of II Peter and of I, II and III John remains uncertain.

II & III John (after AD 90)

These brief letters, one to a church and one to a person, are evidently by the same person as I John, and may well have been written and sent for delivery along with that tract. In contrast to I John, these two seemed to lack enough weighty authority and were not included in the canon until later. The Johannine documents appear to have been written to counteract the influence of Gnosticism, which was growing in the late first century.

> Gnosticism describes ancient religious beliefs that the material world is evil and mankind can be freed from its control only through "enlightenment," believed to be a special gift of revealed knowledge of God.

Jude (after AD 100)

This document was most surely not written by Judas, a brother of Jesus. It is a brief tract, written to warn about those who create divisions and to encourage faithfulness to the faith "once for all entrusted to the saints" (verse 3).

Revelation (AD 95-100)

This document includes letters to seven churches in Asia (southwest Asia Minor around Ephesus) in chapters 2-3. The "letters section" is followed by a dramatic apocalypse in chapters 4-22. The broadest interpretation of the Apocalypse has been that it is a series of visions about the end of time. Attempts have been made in every generation to "solve the secrets" and discover when and how the end of time will come.

I have come to believe that this document is a drama written in highly figurative language during the Domitian persecutions of AD 90-100, which were most severe in Rome and in the Ephesus area.[1] The dramatic visions figuratively described the great conflict of evil against God's people. The writer described, for the encouragement of the suffering Christians, how God would prevail in the end, even if he had to destroy the world to defeat the Roman power and deliver his people. In the end, God would bring his people to a new world of peace. I believe the "prophecies" of the book were meant for the people to believe that they would happen in their own generation as God stood with them and delivered them. What a vision of hope!!! This document was one of the last to be accepted by the churches because of the confusion about its meaning. Its place in the canon has never ceased to be questioned.

Sifting and Sorting as Part of the Canonizing Process

During the second century, more and more written materials were being produced as the Christian movement grew and spread around the Mediterranean basin. Christian communities developed in Antioch of Syria, in Ephesus in Asia Minor, in Macedonia, in Greece, in Alexandria in Egypt, and in Rome. Copies of first-century writings were circulated and collected in groups by churches as they were able to obtain copies. Recognized Christian leaders arose who came to be known as the church fathers. They began to write guidelines for the churches that became a part of the process of evaluating and sifting the growing body of writings. The sifting and sorting process continued for 250 years before a canonized New Testament came to be.

During those two centuries, the documents in our New Testament were being copied by hand. (Remember, the invention of printing was still 1,200 years in the future.) Some of the copying was done by groups of professional scribes, but much of it was done by someone who just made copies for a local church. There were no "authorized" documents or "approved" texts, so the copyists often inserted explanatory notes and sometimes apparently changed the text to make it read as they thought it should.

This raises a question about textual accuracy. No original documents of New Testament books have survived. What we have are the texts resulting from the generations of copying, with some significant variations along the way. These texts have to be evaluated as we try to find the most accurate teachings of the earliest records about our Christian faith. This is the process called textual criticism, a term that describes careful and comparative study by skilled specialists in languages, documents, literature, history, culture, theology and theological controversies. This field of specialization has contributed much to our understanding of the New Testament we read and cherish.

The text of our New Testament comes from copies of copies of copies across many generations, along with translations of translations of those copies. The changing of texts by copyists was known from earliest times.

Origin, who lived before AD 250, wrote, "Differences among the manuscripts have become great, either through the negligence of some copyists or through the perverse audacity of others. They either neglect to check over what they have transcribed, or in the process of checking, they make additions or deletions as they please."[2]

Ireneus, who lived before AD 200, accused Marcion, his contemporary, of "dismembering the epistles of Paul" to take out passages with which he did not agree.[3]

Dionysius, bishop of Corinth before AD 200, complained that "false believers" mutilated his writings and dared to tamper with the word of the Lord himself.[4]

The biblical book of Revelation includes a warning against "adding to" or "removing from" the words of the book (22:18-19). So making changes by copyists was evidently a fairly common practice.

The process of copying, in turn, meant that the changes would tend to become permanent. Once a change had been made in one copy, henceforth all copies would include the changes. Many of the changes were unintentional, and most did not do violence to the text. In 1707, John Mill published the result of thirty years of comparing some 100 Greek manuscripts of the New Testament and quotations from them by writers through the centuries. He identified 30,000 variant readings, and he did not include different word order or a dropped letter from words unless the meaning was changed.[5]

Most of the changes were of no real importance, but theological controversies arose. A doctrine called Docetism developed around the question, "Did Jesus really have a physical human body?" The Docetists believed that the "spiritual Christ" adopted the "physical Jesus" at his baptism and abandoned him just before the crucifixion, so incarnation was never real and the Christ was never truly physical. Gnosticism, another controversial doctrine, held that matter is evil and only special enlightenment can free us from it. Some copyists changed texts to make them agree with what the copyists believed about these and other tenets of faith. There were also changes in the content included in some documents. For instance, the story of the woman taken in adultery in John 7:53-8:11 was not included in the oldest existing manuscripts, and in later copies it was included at different places in the text. In Mark 16, the oldest surviving manuscripts end at verse 8. Later copies included verses 9-20 or some other form of ending for the document.

What can we say, then? We simply do not have exact texts of the original manuscripts of the documents in our New Testament. It is equally true that there is so much overwhelming agreement across the multiple sources that have survived that we can confidently believe that we have a reliable text in our New Testament—reliable records about who Jesus was, about what he did and taught, and also about the early Christians and the early historical rise of the Christian church. Reliable records, yes, but fragmentary and incomplete, and in places inaccurate. We ought not let ourselves be trapped into the untenable position of believing we have to defend every verse of our text of the New Testament as being without human alteration and human error.

The Gathering and Evaluating Process

Of the documents in our New Testament, the letters of Paul were the first written. Since they were letters to the churches he had close association with, it follows that those were the first churches to have copies of his letters. Because of Paul's influence in those churches, they valued and preserved his letters. We have noted how some of the letters were circulated, and it seems clear that the churches kept their originals and made copies to share with others. Thus the process of copying and developing collections of the earliest Christian writings began.

As more written documents were developed through the decades, the churches faced some basic questions. How accurate were the documents? How beneficial were

they for the churches? The early churches tended to answer these questions with two other questions:
1. Did a particular document come from an apostle (an eyewitness of the life of Jesus)?
2. Did a particular document have a quality of inspiration by the Holy Spirit making it appropriate for and edifying to the church for use in public worship?

The initial gathering and evaluating were done by local churches and their leaders, not by groups of bishops or by regional councils—that would come later. The first known reference to a collected group of Christian writings comes from around AD 95 in a letter from Clement of Rome to the church in Corinth, in which he wrote of a collection of the letters of Paul. The four Gospels were written from AD 65-100 and were already known as a collected group by AD 120.

The first known attempt to form a recognized authoritative collection of Christian writings for use in public worship was made by Marcion about AD 150. His collection included ten letters of Paul and the Gospel of Luke. Marcion was a wealthy layman merchant from Sinope on the Asia Minor coast of the Black Sea. He went to Rome and joined the church there in AD 140. Because of a controversy, he was expelled from the church in AD 144. His attempt to define a group of authoritative Christian writings arose as his defense of his position after he was rejected as a heretic. It is easy to believe that his choice of writings by Paul and Luke was swayed by their great influence in Asia Minor, which was his home country.

Around AD 175, Athenagoras of Athens made a collection of the four Gospels and ten of Paul's letters. Around AD 190, Theophilus of Antioch in Syria wrote that the four Gospels were equal in inspiration with the Old Testament Jewish scriptures, and that the letters of Paul were "almost equal." This is the first known written statement evaluating Christian writings as equal with what was the recognized sacredness of the Jewish scriptures. This set Christian writings on the threshold of acceptance as a New Testament.

The process of collecting and evaluating continued during the third century (AD 200-300). Ireneus of Lyons in France, Tertullian of Carthage in North Africa, Clement of Alexandria in Egypt, Origin of Caesarea in Palestine, Hippolytus of Rome, and Eusebius of Caesarea in Palestine all set forth lists of documents that the churches they were associated with accepted as inspired and authoritative for use in worship and teaching.

There was broad agreement in their lists, including the Gospels, Acts, and ten letters of Paul. There was considerable disagreement about whether or not to accept and include the other letters that some attributed to Paul, the General Epistles and Revelation. Several writings were also variably included in or rejected from the lists that did not finally become part of our New Testament, including The Teaching of the Twelve, The Shepherd of Hermas, The Acts of Paul, The Revelation of Peter, and The Letter of Barnabas. Other writings were widely circulated but were almost universally rejected by the churches, including The Gospel of Peter, The Gospel of Thomas, Traditions of Matthias, Acts of Andrew, and Acts of John.

The first surviving record including the exact twenty-seven documents of our New Testament was set forth by Athanasius in AD 367. He was bishop of Alexandria in Egypt, and he declared those twenty-seven books as authoritative for his diocese. There was not universal agreement. The churches in Syria did not accept this canon, and the Eastern Orthodox churches have always maintained and used a slightly different canon.

Church history includes a period of general councils (AD 300-800) that focused primarily on hammering out theological details of Christian faith and teaching. While the canon of the New Testament was debated in the councils, they largely recognized the accepted usage in the churches rather than officially forming the canon of the New Testament.

As the Roman Catholic Church became hierarchical and dominantly powerful in the west, it took control of the Scriptures and restricted them to Latin (the Vulgate translation) until the invention of printing, the Enlightenment, and the Protestant Reformation made the Bible more widely available in German and English translations.

---

[1] Williston Walker, *A History of the Christian Church* (New York: Charles Scribner's Sons, 1950), 34. Martin Rist, "The Revelation," *The Interpretert's Bible*, 12 (1957): 354.
[2] Cited by Bart D. Erhman, *Misquoting Jesus* (New York: Harper Collins, 2005), 52.
[3] Erhman, *Misquoting Jesus*, 53.
[4] Ibid.
[5] Erhman, *Misquoting Jesus*, 83-84.

Major Developments in Traditional Christianity

The First Shaping of Christian Doctrines

The first Christians were Jewish associates of Jesus during the years of his public ministry. They were steeped in the beliefs and practices of Judaism which had developed through the preceding 2,000 years. There are clear evidences in the Gospels that Jesus taught and practiced religious ideas that were different and contrary to the religious traditions of Judaism. The Jewish religious leaders were vocal and determined opponents of what Jesus was teaching and doing. Their opposition led to their insistent demands for his death in an attempt to eliminate his teaching and his influence on the people.

So, those first Christians shared the beliefs about the hoped-for messiah that we find in the Old Testament. The Jewish messianic hope developed as their national life fell under the dominance of other empires, which they believed violated their "chosen nation" status as the covenant people of YaHWeh. The Jews dreamed of a new "son of David" who would arise and be "the anointed one of God (messiah)." He would be enabled and blessed by God to serve as a great monarch, raise an army, throw off the bonds of their oppressors, and raise their nation again to prominence in the world.

Having spent all their previous lives in a culture where messianic hope was a central focus of their religion, the followers of Jesus were confused by things he said about the purpose and end of his life and work. Even after his death and resurrection, his followers are recorded (Acts 1:6) to have asked the risen Christ, "Lord, will you at this time *restore the kingdom to Israel?*" The words of Jesus to Pilate during the Roman trial, "My kingdom is not of this world" (John 18:36), would have been totally different from what the Jews of that day had been taught to believe, including those who had become disciples of Jesus.

The followers who were the first Christians faced a central change in their basic beliefs about Jesus:
- Who was he really?
- What would their religious faith and practice be like now that he was not physically present among them?

- How did they fit their new experiences into their old traditions of Jewish religion?
- What did Pentecost mean in this changing religious picture?

Questions like these had to be worked out among the early Christians as they tried to follow the Lord they had come to believe in and trust. Led by the Holy Spirit of God who had become their new *Paraclete*, they built fellowships of believers and gave public witness about their new faith. The experience of Pentecost caused them to believe that God's Holy Spirit was present with them, just as God's Eternal Son had been with them, and that this was God's new way of being present among them.

Churches developed and organization with leaders became necessary, so elders, deacons (servant ministers) and overseers (bishops) became part of the Christian movement. Documents were written: letters to churches like those of Paul, pamphlets interpreting the meaning of Christianity, records of the remembered words and acts of Jesus. Local groups of Christians formed churches. Later, churches in areas around cities like Antioch in Syria, Alexandria in Egypt, Ephesus in Asia, and Rome in Italy became centers of Christianity, with a central influential leader exercising more and more influence as an overseer (bishop).

The Period of the Early Councils

Beginning in AD 325, a series of councils were held at which groups of bishops and other church leaders worked to agree on creedal statements defining the Christian faith or some doctrine of the faith. There were numerous councils, but some of them have been considered general councils. Consider the significance of the first five councils.[1]

1. The Council of Nicaea in AD 325 was focused on the nature of Jesus and the relation of the Son to the Father. Was the Son of the same "substance" as the Father and thus as eternal, or was the Son of a different "created substance" and thus not as eternal as the Father? The council held that the Son was of the same substance.
2. The Council of Constantinople in AD 381 focused on the "consubstantiality" of the Holy Spirit. Was the Holy Spirit of the "same substance" as the Father and the Son? The council held that the Holy Spirit was "consubstantial" (of the same nature).
3. The Council at Ephesus in AD 431 focused on the relation of the divine and the human in the incarnate Jesus. The council did not solve anything for the churches.

4. The Council at Chalcedon in AD 451 continued the search for an understanding of the relation of the human and the divine in Jesus. This council is noted primarily for the growing struggle between the bishops from eastern and western churches. The council ended with no united voice.
5. A second Council at Constantinople in AD 553 focused on the meaning of Christ's suffering and the question of whether the Father and the Holy Spirit shared in that suffering. Again, the council ended with no united voice.

These councils reflect the kind of questions the early Christians were trying to resolve, for there was no source they could go to for definitive answers. Remember that there was no canonized New Testament for the first 386 years, and even after the New Testament documents were canonized there were no answers to many of their specific questions.

The Establishment of a Hierarchical Church

Another major development in the late sixth century changed the nature of the Christian movement and the Christian Church. From the beginning of the Christian movement, struggles for prominence and pre-eminence arose among men with strong personalities in places of leadership. Bishops of the most influential churches in the most influential cities often had the most clout when it came to settling differences and establishing doctrines of the new Christian faith. By the late sixth century, the Bishop of Rome had become the pre-eminent bishop in the western churches.

Two factors certainly contributed to the Roman bishop's influence:
- Rome was the capitol of the empire.
- The bishops there claimed to be linear followers of the Apostle Peter. (Legend held that he was martyred in that city when Nero was emperor.)

By AD 590, the bishops of Rome had so consolidated their influence and power that Bishop Gregory was elected as pope and the Roman papacy was firmly established. Gregory, who served until his death in AD 604, has been known through history as Pope Gregory I, Gregory the Great.[2]

Through the next four centuries, the Christian movement went through good times and bad. The church expanded in the west (from Palestine through Europe), but declined in the east (from Palestine through the areas where Arab nationalism and Islam, the Muslim religion, developed and expanded). The Roman Church was not an unchallenged monolith under control of the pope. There were struggles with competing bishops and princes. For some, bishoprics became offices sought for position, power and wealth, and were sometimes filled by men of corrupt morals.

Division into Eastern and Western Churches

In AD 1054, competing papal claims by the Bishop of Rome and the Patriarch of Constantinople caused a major schism in the church. The eastern churches declared their allegiance to the Patriarch of Constantinople. The Eastern Orthodox Church and the national Orthodox churches of Asia were born. The western churches stayed committed to the Bishop of Rome as the Roman Catholic Pope. This separation continues to the present day.[3]

The Dissenter Factor

Through the centuries there were dissenter movements, groups who did not accept the authority of the pope and followed their own expressions of Christian faith and practice. There were prominent dissenter movements in the 14th and 15th centuries in England and in the eastern European countries of Bohemia and Moravia. The first English translations of the New Testament, along with groups known as the Quakers, the Moravians, the Anabaptists, and other Pietists, came out of these movements.

The Protestant Reformation

The corruption and excesses of the Roman Catholic Church became more evident as Europe emerged from the Dark Ages. A renaissance of learning began to take hold, and the spread of information was enhanced by Gutenberg's invention of the printing press. In AD 1517, a Roman monk named Martin Luther posted on the church door at Wittenberg, Germany, a statement of 95 items (theses) he wanted to challenge in debates with the Roman hierarchy. The pope demanded that he recant. Luther refused. The pope excommunicated Luther, and the Protestant Reformation began.[4] It spread throughout Europe, and ever since, western Christianity has been characterized by Roman Catholic and Protestant faiths. The non-Catholic movement in western Christianity has developed into the multiple Protestant and evangelical denominations that are present throughout the world.

---

[1]John A. Hardon, "Councils of the Church," *Collier's Encyclopedia*, 7 (1987): 394-395. B. K. Kuiper, *The Church in History* (Grand Rapids: Wm. B. Erdman's Publishing Co., 1951), 72-76.

[2]Williston Walker, *A History of the Christian Church* (New York: Charles Scribner's Sons, 1950), 190-192. Kuiper, *The Church in History*, 100-101.

[3]Lars P. Qualben, *A History of the Christian Church* (New York: Thomas Nelson and Sons, 1951), 161-163. Walker, *A History of the Christian Church*, 224-225.

[4]Qualben, *A History of the Christian Church*, 232-237.

Seeking a Personal Faith

With a historical summary of the development of religious thought and practice across the centuries of human history set forth, let us try now to put it all into perspective and find our way to a personal faith. We begin with a summary of some basic traditional Christian beliefs to help establish our focus.

A Summary of Some Traditional Beliefs

People Are Created in the Image of God

Numerous and varied ideas have been held about the meaning of the phrase.
- Some have held that "the image of God" refers to physical likeness and support that idea with references to anthropomorphic expressions in the Bible (eyes of God, hand of God, God walking, God speaking, etc.).
- Some believe it refers to our moral consciousness. (God is the determiner of good and evil, and we have a sense of good and evil.)
- Some think the phrase refers to our human spirituality—that God is spirit, and our spiritual soul is our likeness to God.
- Others have held that our image of God is in:
    - Our ability to reason. God is the supreme designer, and people are able to think and plan.
    - Our sociability. God engages in relationships, and people are social beings.
    - Our volitional self-determination. God acts by both permissive and determinative will, and people have the capacity to make choices and act on them.

I have come to believe that we need to "coin a phrase" to describe what it means to have in us the "image of God." The description I use is that God is "SPIRIT/PERSON" (all uppercase and bold because God is infinite in every way), and humans are "spirit/persons" (all lowercase to indicate that we are finite).

We need to start with God. The "image of God in man" must refer to what there is in human nature that is like God, not what in God is like human nature.

All religious concepts have held that the "Supreme" is non-physical, and that "material" came into being by some supernatural cause. Even religious systems that focused on material objects (nature, animals, carved idols, etc.) had at their basis a belief that "divine spirits" inhabiting those objects were what was being worshipped, not the physical object. The worship of Jesus of Nazareth in Christianity has not been the worship of a human person who achieved divinity. The worship of Jesus is the worship of the eternal Son of God who became incarnate (eternal spirit who took on human form and became a fully human person).

There is a deep conviction in humanity that there is a quality in us that is not present in other life forms. This distinctive feature is not in our physical mammalian bodies (we are really quite alike with pigs in body). It is not in the life principle that sustains existence from birth until physical death, after which the body decays. The unique thing about human persons is the spirit that exists as a conscious self. We believe we have a spiritual nature like God.

This belief is a matter of faith. It can't be proven in a lab, for lab tests deal only with physical entities. Spirit is non-physical, and we believe that God is supreme eternal spirit.

We also believe that God is person. Personhood is a distinctive state of being that some religious systems believe is true of the "Supreme." This concept is central to the Hebrew and Christian faiths.

The concept of personhood has distinctive features inherent in its very nature:
- Consciousness of self
- Capacity to relate to others
- Capacity to reason and design
- Capacity to care about others
- Capacity to aspire and seek
- Capacity to make choices and act on them

The Hebrew and Christian faiths believe that the "Supreme" has, and acts on, all of these features of personal nature. And these two religious faiths believe that human persons, however they have come into being (by direct creation or ageless evolution), have been made by the "Supreme Maker" of all things to have the inherent nature of personhood, with its distinctive features. Those features in human persons correspond finitely to the features that belong to the supreme nature of God infinitely.

So if we posit a faith that the "Supreme" entity is a SPIRIT/PERSON who is infinite in nature and character, *and* if we take seriously the idea that human persons were "created" in the "image of God," *then* we can believe that there are fundamental features in our nature and character like corresponding features in the nature and character of God. The fundamental difference between human persons and God is that in humans both nature and character are finite, while everything in God is infinite.

Therefore, if we posit a faith that God is SPIRIT/PERSON (uppercase because infinite), we can describe humans as spirit/persons (lowercase because finite). This, in turn, provides a beginning basis for trying to understand the nature of our relationship to God, and to understand the meaning and consequences of "the fall of man."

People Are Sinful

We need to begin with a question about origins. Were one man and one woman created as fully moral human persons by God in one specific action? This is the traditional Christian understanding of the Genesis account. Or are the two creation stories in Genesis figurative parables about eons-long evolution from simple to complex, resulting in the development of a species of human persons with the nature of spirit/persons, having in finite measure features that parallel infinite features in the nature and character of the Creator God?

A second question: Are human persons capable of harmony with God or alienation from God? And is this harmony or alienation the result of acceptance of or rebellion against the inescapable Sovereign Creator/subject creature relationship between the "Maker" and the "made"?

The creation stories in the book of Genesis can be understood in more than one way. The one you choose to believe does not determine whether or not you are a faithful believer in the inspiration of the Bible. Records of historical events, figurative metaphors, similitudes, poetry and dramas are all prominent in the Bible and are readily believed to be revelations of great eternal truths. A very basic matter in Bible study as you approach any passage is to let the Bible speak to you; do not simply accept someone else's understanding and interpretation. Your faith needs to become *your* faith.

Another basic question we need to ask as we try to understand what it means to be a "sinner" is, "What was the nature of the experience called the 'Fall'?" That question leads to other questions such as, "How literal do you believe the record of the Garden of Eden and the events of the 'Fall' are?" "What is the meaning of 'the tree of the knowledge of good and evil'?" (Genesis 3:5). "What is the meaning of 'the tree of life'?" (Genesis 3:22)?

We also need to ask ourselves what we understand to be the nature of the temptation: "What was God withholding from them? What was God cheating them out of?" This certainly seems to be what was going on in Eve's mind, and it is clear that the writer of the story believed that moral humans have consciousness of a relationship with God, the ability to reason, and freedom of choice.

And there is the question, "What did they do?" How do you "eat" of a figurative tree? Was their "disobedience" the exercising of their free will to choose independence from God as they tried to find satisfaction of their wants, instead of trusting that their creaturehood under God's sovereignty would bring fullness of life?

However you choose to answer these questions, it is clearly evident from human experience and awareness that we are all sinful, that there is a dysfunction of some nature in the relationship of humans and God.

The Consequences of Sinfulness

Now a question of truly historic consequence: "What was the result of the 'Fall'?" "Did the 'Fall' make people mortal?" Would humans have died if "Adam and Eve" had not sinned? Paul wrote, "As sin came into the world through one man and death through sin, and so death spread to all men because all men sinned" (Romans 5:12). This idea assumes a single original created couple and a single original sinful act which caused death and corrupted all humanity.

The Genesis passage includes the statement, "You shall not eat of the tree in the midst of the garden, nor shall you touch it, lest you die" (Genesis 2:17, 3:3). Does this reference to death mean physical death or spiritual death? I understand spiritual death to mean alienation from God, which means to be "at odds" with ultimate reality and out of sync with the supreme power, wisdom and goodness.

This matter has been debated throughout Christian history as the question, "Did the 'Fall' destroy 'the image of God in man'?" If we are correct that "the image of God in man" is the SPIRIT/PERSON-spirit/person correlation, then human sinfulness did not change that essential nature of human persons.

The traditional belief through the centuries has been that the "Fall" did corrupt the total human posterity of Adam. Before Jesus lived, Judaism had already come to believe that sin and guilt came upon the human race through Adam's "Fall," and that humankind is absolutely unable to free itself from it. It is widely believed that this is what Paul believed and wrote. This understanding of the meaning of the "Fall" continued to be set forth by the defining church leaders up through the Protestant Reformation. Tertullian (AD 150-225) wrote that the moral depravity resulting from Adam's disobedience passed through procreation to the entire race. (His phrase was "infected from his seed.")[1] Ambrose (AD 340-397) wrote that through the "Fall" we are born as sinners, sin being an attribute that belongs to us from our conception.[2] Pelagius (AD 350-400) refuted that position as absurd, contending that sinfulness is by act of the will. The church leaders in the west condemned him as a heretic.[3] Augustine (AD 350-430) wrote, "Lust comes from a perverse will" and "Evil in the world is a result of freedom." But according to Augustine, God controls the will, which is fated by predestined election before birth. So Augustine believed the individual was fated with sinfulness before any effect of procreation could occur. He wrote, "Man can believe, but only God can give him the power to believe."[4] That

Seeking a Personal Faith

is no freedom at all. The Council of Ephesus (AD 431) determined that Augustine prevailed over Pelagius in the faith of the churches in the west.[5]

Duns Scotus (AD1265-1308) wrote that since humankind by nature has sensuous impulses along with reason and will, there is in humankind by nature an inward rebellion. Original sin was to him a lack of natural original righteousness.[6] (So sin is really God's fault because of faulty original design.)

William of Occam (AD 1300-1350) maintained that the "infection" of natural sensuous rebellion against the spirit has been passed from parent to child (Adam to all humankind) by procreation (his phrase—"the generating act").[7]

Martin Luther (AD 1483-1546) agreed with Augustine against Pelagius that "through the act of generation that is performed in evil lust, sin has passed from parents to their children."[8] (So the very foundation of human reproduction is evil.)

The Anabaptist Huldrich Zwingli (AD 1484-1531) held that human disobedience was sin, which shattered the original nature of humankind, who had been created free and innocent. The descendants of the original sinners are sinful because they inherit a shattered nature.[9]

John Calvin (AD 1509-1564) held that sinful character was passed to posterity by inheritance ("from a corrupt root has sprung corrupt branches").[10] This was by divine appointment—it was God's will that it should be so.

The Council of Trent (AD 1545-1563) held that the first man lost the righteousness of his original created nature and came under the wrath of God and the power of the devil. The whole man (body and soul) was changed for the worse. Free will was perverted. This corruption of nature then passed to posterity by propagation, not by imitation.[11] (So sinfulness is inborn, not learned).

So, we face a major question: Is sin a spiritual and moral matter of the will and freedom of choice, or is the sinful nature of human persons a physical, sexually caused inherited condition? Were humans originally non-sexual, and was "becoming sexual" the real meaning of the first disobedience and the origination of sinfulness? Did the "Fall" result in the "total depravity" of the human race?

As noted above, Judaism held that humans could do "absolutely nothing to free themselves" from the corrupted nature and guilt of sinfulness. Augustine, Luther and Calvin all understood Paul to teach this, and they held that everything is of the omnipotent will of God, whether anyone should "will or not will," and this was foreordained for every person. Luther wrote that "man is free only to do evil."[12] Calvin wrote that "the cause of the contagion lies neither in the substance of the flesh, nor in that of the soul, but because it has been ordained by God."[13]

E.Y. Mullins interpreted "total depravity" to mean that "all parts of our nature" have been affected by sin. According to Mullins, this does not mean that all humans are as bad as they can be, nor that all are equally bad, nor that humankind has no morally good impulses; however, it does mean that humankind cannot change its own nature or radically alter the bias of its will toward sinful choices and sinful actions.[14]

What I Believe

I believe that every person begins as if he or she were at the Garden of Eden, and that every person is by God's grace a spirit-person, bearing in very nature the finite image of the infinite God. I believe that every person has the capability of fellowship with or alienation from a relationship of harmony with God, and that every person is gifted with the abilities of reason, choice and free will. I believe that temptation arises out of the arrogance of a creature who dares to think that self-determination is better than harmony with Creator through trust and obedience. (See James 1:14-15.) I believe that alienation and "lostness" occur when a person chooses to attempt independence from God in the values and choices and actions of life. I believe that each person, as he or she matures to a grasp of right and wrong, must and does make free choice of what and whom to believe in, and what value system to trust and pursue in life.

People Can Be Saved

What does all of this mean for a person today who is concerned about his or her standing with God? This question leads into a discussion of the gospel of faith, repentance, conversion, and new birth/regeneration—and the meaning of "salvation."

The terms "lost" and "saved" are being used here in a religious sense, not in a physical sense (as in "a sheep that wandered astray" or "a coin that is misplaced" or "money banked away in plans for future use").

It seems clear that "lostness" means alienation from and disharmony with God caused by choosing value systems that are out of sync with the spiritual and moral values God established through creation (because they are the values that reside at the heart of his character). It follows, then, that "to be made right with God" requires a transformed change in spiritual and moral values as a chosen and followed way of life.

Can that transformed change become a reality? How can it happen? What part does God play, and what part does a person play?

It is a central tenet of the Christian faith that a person can be saved. Underlying that faith is the Christian belief in the loving, forgiving character of God and the incarnate mission of the eternal Son of God. Seeking to grasp and understand these fundamentals is the purpose of the following discussion.

Fundamentals of Faith about Salvation

The history of human thought about the meaning of salvation and the means of salvation has been long and involved. Many threads of thought, faith and practice have been woven into the varied streams of religious development through the centuries dealing with sinful people, how people seek relief from the consequences of their sinfulness, and how they can gain the favor of their God. These aspects of our relationship to God need to be summarized as a part of our search for a personal faith about salvation.

In this section, I will set forth ideas I hold and some things I have come to believe, understanding that some of these ideas are not the traditional tenets that have developed through church history in Christian theology. I do not ask that you accept these ideas because you think kindly of me; I ask only that you give these ideas careful examination as *you* decide what *you* really believe. Your faith does need to be *your* faith.

The following pages review some foundational ideas that I believe:

- The Supreme Being of all that exists is infinite and eternal. A wonderfully basic truth about God was revealed to Moses in his "burning bush" experience in the personal name of God. The word in the Hebrew text is *eheyeh* (first person singular of *hayah*, the verb "to be") and is generally translated in English as "I Am." I believe this is a clear indication of God's intention to reveal to humankind that the Supreme Being is self-existent, non-created, and personal in nature. Inherent in the nature and character of the Supreme Being is the ultimate ideal of all that could possibly exist. Therefore, all that has come into existence is the result of the wisdom, choice and action of that Supreme Being, called variously *El* or *Allah* or God.
- God (the Supreme, uncreated, self-existing Being and source of all else that exists) chose to create a material universe. There is evidence, which seems to be reliable based on the current state of scientific research, that God caused a material universe to come into existence through a process of eons-long evolution, and to develop into a complex system of planets and galaxies. This universe includes the earth, which has physical conditions that have supported the origin and development of many species of living things, including the human race.
- The universe God established is a moral universe, and human beings are moral persons. This means that an individual's every idea, feeling, motive or action is either good or better or

> **Animistic religion** is the belief that certain animals are sacred and inhabited by supernatural powers.
>
> **Natural object religion** is the belief that supernatural powers are present in heavenly objects, rivers, trees, etc.

best, or bad or worse or worst. These moral qualities are measured by their likeness to or variance from the ultimate ideals inherent in the nature and character of God.
- In the material universe, the most highly developed species of God's evolutionary work is the species called human persons. Human persons have a four-fold nature: physical, mental, emotional and spiritual.
    - Human physical existence (shared with other mammals) begins with potentiality at conception; develops through gestation to birth; grows, matures and reproduces; and declines to infirmity, dies and decays.
    - Human mental capacity develops in the brain through experience, memory, thought and reason—beginning at birth and ending (insofar as we know) at physical death.
    - Human emotional experience has to do with feelings, including our attraction to or revulsion from the pleasantness or offensiveness of any thought or experience, resulting from the circumstances of our lives.
    - Human spiritual nature is the inner non-physical being of an individual encompassing the personal sense of self, of personhood, and of relationship to God.
- This fully human personhood could exist only after the long evolutionary process by which God brought into being a species with the physical, mental, emotional and spiritual capacities to function in each of these areas of human life and relationships.

    The evolutionary development of the human species from the simple primitive to what we call advanced and civilized included the origin and development of religious thought, systems and institutions.
- Religious thought had its beginning when humans developed to the stage that they had awareness of something supernatural—uncontrollable forces, unexplainable events and unanswerable questions.

This level of religious understanding and practice is reflected in the primitive animistic religions and the natural object religions. These religions originated before people came to think of the Supreme Being as having personal characteristics, a stage of religious development that can be identified as beginning about the time of the rise of Hebrew religion (c. 2000 BC).

Through many ideas and stages, there developed a concept of God as a universal supreme spirit who has inherent in character the qualities of personhood (i.e. God thinks, plans, feels, desires, wills, acts.)

After eighteen millennia (20,000-2,000 BC) of developing religious thought, the concept arose that human persons share a nature and moral character with the

Supreme Person. God is in nature an *infinite* "SPIRIT-PERSON." God has caused the human species, created in his image, to develop as *finite* "spirit-persons."

The human species came to believe that our creaturely relation to the Supreme Being as creator makes us subject to the pleasure or displeasure of the deity being worshipped, and that the deity favors or disfavors us because of our actions. As people later came to think of God as personal, they also came to believe, through their self-awareness and ability to reason and question, that they have freedom of will and the ability to choose to obey or disobey God, and to be faithful or unfaithful to God's claim on their lives.

In Hebrew and Christian theology, this level and focus of religious understanding is reflected in the inspired parables in the beginning of the book of Genesis in the Hebrew Old Testament Scriptures. These beautiful stories reflect an evolutionary development in the natural universe from simple to complex, the final level of species development being human persons who share the personal nature and character of God. These stories also reflect the reasons we see dysfunction (called sinfulness) in the relationship between human persons and the Lord God.

All of this, in turn, raises the question of the meanings of lostness (disharmony) and salvation (reconciliation and restoration of harmony). These two religious concepts run as threads through both Hebrew and Christian sacred writings as they are found in the Christian Bible. This discussion of the fundamental meaning of relationship and status between the Supreme God and human persons who have freedom of will is based on the following basic beliefs:

- God is infinite, eternal, unchanging, personal and moral, and has inherent in his character all that is ideal of good versus bad, improving versus worsening, and lasting versus passing.
- Humans have an I-thou (Person-to-person) relationship with God in contrast to everything else in the physical universe, which has an I-it (Person-to-thing) relationship to God.
- In the I-it relationship of Creator to creation, everything in the physical universe, with the single exception of the human species, is controlled by divinely established natural law or species instinct.
- People are able to share in an I-thou relationship with God because he has graciously caused us to develop with capacities to reason, question, will, choose and act. This is the inherent meaning of being persons instead of merely mammalian animals.
- The "competence of the human soul under God"[15] means that God, in choosing to "raise up" a species of moral persons, chose to take the risk that humans would disagree as well as agree, disobey as well as obey, say "no" as well as "yes," and choose bad as well as good. The option to choose disobedience is what makes choosing obedience a meaningful part of an I-thou

relationship. The option to scorn is what makes a choice to love so precious between persons.

In answer to the question of the fundamental meaning of "lostness," traditional Judeo-Christianity has adhered to the following train of thought and belief:

> The first humans were placed in an edenic paradise of innocence. They were tempted by a serpent (generally understood to be Satan) to distrust and disobey God, and they yielded to temptation. God expelled them from Eden and condemned them to laborious work and painful childbirth as punishment for their disobedience. This sin alienated them from God and caused them to become vulnerable to physical death. This beginning of sinfulness so corrupted all their descendants that "original sin" has destined all humanity to condemnation and to eternal hell unless and until redeemed by the atoning sacrifice of Jesus by crucifixion and acceptance of that vicarious penalty to satisfy the offended justice of God.

This traditional course of understanding and belief involves several ideas that raise questions for serious students of the religious history involved.

First, it is based on belief that the human species began with the direct creation of two full-grown persons, male and female, who had perfect innocence but apparently no sexual awareness of their gender difference, not even their nakedness. This is in contrast to belief that the human species evolved over eons of time to the stage of personal awareness, rational thought, moral consciousness and religious perception.

Second, traditional Christianity developed out of the belief that "original sin" so ruined the "image of God in man" that human persons could not choose any moral way except evil until they "received salvation through Jesus." This is in contrast to belief that the "image of God in man" means that, in essential nature, human persons have a "spiritual dimension" that corresponds to the truth that God is infinite, eternal, supreme, divine spirit. If human persons are indeed "finite spirit-persons" as God is "infinite SPIRIT-PERSON," then the "image of God in man" is not destroyed by sinfulness. Instead, sinfulness means that humans misuse their freedom of choice in ways that cause disharmony and alienation in the I-Thou (person-to-person) relationship that exists between the eternal God and every individual.

Third, the understanding of evil temptation in traditional Christianity comes from belief that an evil demigod (Satan) is in competition against a good God. It has long been considered heretical to question this tenet of faith. This understanding of evil, however, needs to be re-examined against some changes that have occurred in the development of human thought about religion. Such a study cannot proceed without our making choices individually about how we understand the Bible. Earlier chapters about the origins of our scriptural documents and their canonization into a book held sacred by Christian believers has included the information here reviewed.

Documentary evidence has convinced me that before about the tenth century BC, the prevailing belief about good and evil was that both came from the same source—the favor or disfavor of the deity under whose control a person or a people lived. During the period we know in Hebrew history as the Babylonian Exile, a marked change occurred.

The understanding of good and evil shifted from having a single source (moral monism) to having two sources (moral dualism). Persian Zoroastrianism and post-exilic Judaism included belief in a demigod (Persian Angra Mainyu or Shaitin, Hebrew Satan) as the source of evil and the temptation to evil. This change to moral dualism is reflected in the Garden of Eden parable, which I believe to be a part of the post-exilic editing of the Mosaic documents into the form that came down to us. It is also reflected in the references to Satan in Chronicles, Job and Zechariah, which are all post-exilic documents. A connection is also made to Lucifer, who is referred to in some translations of Isaiah 14 as a fallen angel. It is well established that post-exilic Judaism included belief in a demigod (Satan) as the source of evil. This belief has continued in traditional Christianity.

A fundamental question needs to be asked, however. Does evil come from influences outside us (the disfavor of our deity or the temptation of a demigod), or is it a function of the gift of free will which God has caused to develop in the human species to enable an I-Thou relationship? To grapple with this question, it is enlightening to go back to the story of the Garden of Eden. What really caused the people of that parable to wind up "at outs" with God?

The dynamic of the event described in the parable seems to be an unwillingness on the part of the people to accept their creaturehood under the sovereignty of the Creator and to trust God's guidance to bring a fulfilling happiness to life. There is an inspired insight in this wonderful story. One of the good things that God caused to develop in human persons as they evolved to the level of rational beings capable of freedom of choice was the character trait of aspiration. The desire to improve, to achieve something significant, has been at the root of human striving which has led to the development of civilization, the pursuit of learning, and scientific and technological advances.

One danger in aspiration, however, is that it may easily become obsessive ambition, and achievement may give rise to arrogance. This is at the heart of the human action described in the story of Eden. Consider the inspired truth of James 1:14: "Each person is tempted when he is lured and enticed by his own desires" (RSV); "The temptation to give in to evil comes from us and only us. We have no one to blame but the leering, seducing flare-up of our own lust."[16] The attraction of the "tree of the knowledge of good and evil" was the aspiration to be wise and choose for oneself a course to pursue in search of happiness.

That aspiration becomes evil when it ignores the consequences of moral choices and sets us in arrogant distrust of God, who created a moral universe. Love is better than hate, kindness is better than cruelty, generosity is better than greed, peace is better than conflict, faithfulness is better than treachery. To ignore these truths is to show distrust and arrogant contempt for God, as Adam and Eve did. This is the nature of sinfulness and the cause of human divergence and alienation from God. Adam and Eve were expelled from Eden not because God was angry with them, but because they no longer belonged there. This is what it means to be "lost." Lostness is not a status of judgment and condemnation. Lostness is an alienation in relationship caused by wrong choices of value and distrust of person. It can well be called "separation from God."

What Does Salvation Mean, and How Are People Saved?

Through ages of experience there has been a dysfunctional relationship between human persons and the Supreme Being we call God. We call it sinfulness. We experience it as a sense of disobedient rebellion against God's sovereign will. It makes us feel guilty and alienates us from harmony and fellowship with God. How can this fractured relationship be corrected? How can we "be saved" and "made right with God"?

In traditional Christian teaching, the "way of salvation" goes like this: God loves sinful people, but his commitment to justice means that their sinful rebellion must be punished for justice to be satisfied. Sinful people could not earn enough merit to outweigh the guilt of their sinfulness, so if God wanted them to be saved there would have to be a way to "pay the price" to satisfy the demand for justice before the guilt of sinfulness could be removed.

In primitive religions, there developed the belief that people could please their deity by burning offerings on altars to show their gratitude, such as offering the first products gathered at the beginning of harvest (the "first fruits" described in the Hebrew Old Testament). They also believed they could show their devotion to their deity or assuage the displeasure or anger of their deity by burning in sacrifice something of great value to them (such as their best lamb, their prize bull or even their first son, as some of the Baal worshipping tribes did in Canaan). The ancient Hebrews, as well as their tribal neighbors, believed burnt sacrifices and offerings were ways to please God and gain atonement for sin.

The "sacrifice for sin" idea was carried forward into Christian belief by the disciples and early Christians. Since people needed a sacrifice that was great enough to satisfy the justice required by God to atone for their sinfulness and could not gain it by their own merit, God "sent his Son" in the person of Jesus to die on the cross and provide atonement. Because God is loving, he will graciously forgive sinners who will accept the sacrifice of Jesus on their behalf and accept his salvation by faith.

Underlying this belief about sacrifice for sin is the conviction written in Hebrew 10:4, "It is impossible that the blood of bulls and goats should take away sins." However, the sacrifice of Jesus and the shedding of his blood on the cross is believed to be a sufficient sacrifice because of his perfect merit.

This central doctrine of traditional Christianity needs to be carefully examined, for as with numerous ideas of religious understanding, the Bible "does not speak with a single voice" on a variety of subjects, and salvation is one of them.

The question of how good a sacrifice had to be to satisfy the requirements of the deity being worshipped arose as early as the time of the Hebrew patriarchs (2000-1800 BC). Hebrew religion included the requirement that an animal must be "without blemish" to be acceptable to God. Some Canaanites believed that the sacrifice of a child would surely impress their Baal. Abraham even came to believe that the sacrifice of his son Isaac was necessary to satisfy a requirement of God. One of the great mountain-peak moments of revelation was when God made Abraham realize that human sacrifice was not the price of obedience to him.

A period of great advance in religious enlightenment among the Hebrews came in the eighth century BC and is reflected in the writings of Amos, Hosea, Isaiah and Micah. Amos preached that God requires justice in people's relationships, Hebrew and non-Hebrew alike. Hosea preached that unfaithfulness to God is a violation of covenant relationship as surely as adultery is in a marriage. Isaiah heralded the truth that there is only one God and that other presumed deities were creations of people's imaginations. And the truth broke upon the soul of Micah that rightness with God cannot come by anything outside a person (sacrificed animals and rivers of oil—Micah 6:7). Only by a transformed change in values resulting in a change in conduct that leads to doing justice, loving kindness and walking humbly with God (6:8) can people meet what God requires. This revealed insight reversed the belief in blood sacrifice as the means of becoming "right with God."

I find significant differences between the attitude and teachings of Jesus about his death and our salvation as they are reflected in the Gospels, and the interpretations of his death and our salvation written in other New Testament documents and early Christian writings.

The Question of Limited Atonement

Did Jesus, by his death and resurrection, open a way of salvation for all persons who would respond in faith? Or was the work of Christ a limited atonement, done only for the elect, and open only to them because they were the only ones who could respond in faith because God had so predestined both the elect and the non-elect?

Belief in a limited atonement and limited access to the love and care of God has had a long history. We find it first in the Judeo-Christian religion in the Hebrews' understanding of themselves as God's covenant people. This understanding arose from the polytheistic religious environment in which the Hebrews as a people developed.

The Hebrews had a strong sense that Abraham and his descendants were chosen to be a select people with a special covenant relationship with God. They believed that other people around them had their relationships with other deities, most often identified in the Old Testament as the agricultural and fertility deities called Baal and Ashtaroth. The Hebrew religious faith was that God cared about them and the land of Canaan. The rest of the peoples and other lands were under the care of other deities. This limited idea of relationship with God is reflected clearly in the Old Testament. While the Hebrews were instructed to be kind to "the stranger among you," the alien could become an object of God's care and a part of the covenant people only by being circumcised and keeping the law of Moses (i.e., by becoming a Hebrew proselyte).

In the early development of Christianity, the idea of limited atonement and election to God's favor and grace is most clearly stated in the teaching of Paul in Romans 8-9, where the doctrines of foreknowledge, election and predestination are rooted. This belief in limited atonement was advanced in Christian history by Augustine of Hippo. He believed that grace is limited to the elect and predestined, for whom grace is irresistible. The influence of Augustine prevailed in the medieval Roman Catholic Church and in much of the Protestant Reformation.

For Christianity in America, the belief in limited atonement has primarily come from the writings of John Calvin and those who have interpreted and expanded his teachings. A twentieth-century statement of this doctrine is set forth under the acronym TULIP (Total depravity, Unconditional election, Limited atonement, Irresistible grace, and Perseverance of the saints).

- Belief in total depravity grows out of a premise that the image of God in humankind was obliterated in the "Fall" (the sin of Adam and Eve), and this depravity has ever since been passed to all humans by genetic inheritance. People can be restored to approval only by the grace of God in salvation/atonement (or by the sacrament of baptism, as believed in some branches of Christianity).
- Unconditional election is the belief that God *chose* from eternity those for whom Christ would die, those who would respond to the Gospel and have faith, and those who would not. Election is believed to be a divine choice

that is in no way conditioned by anything the individual can do. This is the most fundamental belief in the doctrine of predestination.
- Limited atonement is the belief that Jesus died only for the elect. Since the non-elect had no possibility of redemption, there was no reason for them to be included in the atoning work of Jesus.
- Irresistible grace is the belief that the elect cannot and will not resist the grace of God, so their predestined redemption and glorification is inevitable.
- Perseverance of the saints holds that once the elect have embraced God's grace, they cannot and will not fall from grace to become alienated from God and lose their salvation.

The doctrine of limited atonement has had its dissenters. In every generation of Christian history, there have been those who believed that "whosoever will may come," that God's grace is freely offered to each individual as a gift of love that can be accepted through faith or rejected, and that the death of Jesus was effective atonement for any and all who would believe, repent, trust and accept his saving grace.

This belief in inclusive atonement was expressed by Pelagius in the fifth century, and by Jacob Arminius and the Pietists and Anabaptists in the sixteenth and seventeenth centuries. Denominationally, the limited atonement doctrine has been held in western Christianity by the Calvinist Reformed, Lutheran and Presbyterian churches, and by some Baptist and other congregational church groups. Baptists have tended to hold a middle position, neither fully Arminian nor fully Calvinist.

Baptists generally do not reject the biblical teaching of election but hold that God elected and predestined the *way* redemption would take place (by the faith of a person accepting the grace of salvation). However, God did not determine by divine fiat the choice each individual person would make to accept or reject the atoning work and salvation accomplished and offered by Jesus.

The Priesthood Question

Another question asks, "Does God relate to humans person-to-person, or does God work through mediating priests to give knowledge of himself and dispense his grace to humanity?" The Old Testament reflects a clearly established and hereditary priesthood, begun with the anointing of Aaron and continuing throughout the history of the Hebrew nation. The question of a hierarchical priesthood or the priesthood of all believers rests primarily on interpretations by early church fathers and by an understanding and application of the words of Jesus in Matthew 16:15-19.

The Roman Catholic and Eastern Orthodox branches of Christianity, and the church denominations that have followed their lead, have maintained the hierarchical mediating priesthood doctrine that Jesus made Simon Peter his priestly vicar on earth and committed to him the authority to dispense grace through sacraments and to grant or deny absolution of sin.

The doctrine of the priesthood of all believers is based on the understanding that faith in Jesus as Son of God incarnate is the foundation ("rock") on which the church is built, and that every believer has direct access to God without need for a priest to mediate between them. This position is clearly stated in I Timothy 2:5: "There is one God, and there is one mediator between God and men, the man Christ Jesus."

It seems to me, however, that belief in the competency of every human to respond to God in direct personal access and relationship has been understood and practiced too individualistically by those of us in the free church stream of Christianity. It is an incredible privilege that God created us as persons capable of receiving inspiration and enlightenment from him and responding through free choice of will to trust him or to deny his sovereign lordship in our lives. This awesome privilege of personal relationship with God has inherent within it responsibilities that reach beyond ourselves as individuals. This responsibility is reflected in the concept of priesthood, as in the priesthood of all believers. The well-established role of a priest in Hebrew, Christian and most other religions is that of a person who is qualified and authorized to perform religious rituals. Even more basic, a priest stands between God and people as an intermediary to minister to each on behalf of the other, to speak for God to the people, and to offer sacrifices to God for the people.

The priesthood of the believer, therefore, includes not only the privilege of personal access to and relationship with God as a believer, but also the responsibility to be a witness for God. Each believer is responsible to share the good news of God's love, grace and forgiveness with those who are not believers, and through intercessory prayer to bring others before God with entreaty for his works of grace and mercy in their lives.

The "Covenant People" Question

The questions of limited or universal inclusion in God's redemptive purpose, and of direct or mediated access and relationship with God, raise for me a question about the role of "covenant people" which has such a prominent place in the Old Testament.

The identification of the descendants of Abraham as "covenant people" was established when Abraham sensed a call from God to leave home and kin to become a new nation devoted to the new God (see Genesis 12:1-3).

It should be noted that a "covenant" is a binding agreement or contract between two or more people. A covenant involves what each party to a contract will put into the relationship—that is, what each will and will not do. Covenants may be established between equals or between superiors and subordinates. The concept of "covenant people" in the Bible is a superior/subordinate contract between Creator God and created people, between Sovereign Lord and subject creatures.

The covenant to which God called Abraham involved both privilege and responsibility. The privilege was a special relationship that would exist between God and the descendants of Abraham. God would guide and bless them and make them a great nation. They were to obey God's laws and not worship any other deities. As with every covenant, both sides had to be faithful to the conditions of the agreement or the contract would be breached and the covenant broken.

The responsibility that came with that special relationship with God was to be a channel through which "all the families of the earth would be blessed." This part of what it meant to be "covenant people" raises a significant question: Was it always true that "God so loved the world …"? The Old Testament reflects that many (if not most) Hebrews did not believe that the God they worshipped (YaHWeH) cared about non-Hebrew people the way he cared about them. This fit with the widely held belief that there was an integral relation between the many polytheistic deities and certain areas of land and the people who lived there. To the people, this meant that Yahweh was the God of Canaan and of the Hebrews who lived there as his covenant people. The Egyptian deities were the gods of Egypt and the Egyptian people. The Babylonian deities were the gods of Babylon and the Babylonian people. To the Hebrews, it followed that the non-Hebrew tribes should be driven out of Canaan because it was Yahweh's land but they were not Yahweh's people. Yahweh's land belonged to Yahweh's people. So, while the Hebrews were commanded, "You shall not wrong a *stranger* (alien) or oppress him" (Exodus 22:21), the prevailing attitude among the Hebrews was that they had no responsibility to fulfill that part of the covenant with Abraham about being a channel for the blessing of all nations.

The roles of covenant people and the priesthood of believers include both privilege and responsibility. The privilege is that of direct access and special relationship with God. The responsibility is an obligation to serve others by helping them come to know the love and grace of God and the openness into that love and grace for all people of faith. The responsibility is to serve God by living out a faithful discipleship and by being witnesses of his good news of love and grace to others.

A Different Look at the Meaning of Salvation

All of the above intertwining of covenant, sacrificial offerings, atonement, election, priestly function and substitutionary merit are threads of faith that have arisen and been woven together through four millennia of developing religious thought, experience and practice. In their many varied formulations, they have become "the doctrines of salvation." I believe the whole concept of "salvation" needs to be rethought as guided by the teachings of Jesus in the Gospels.

Three facets of truth seem evident to me from my study of the Gospels:
1. Human salvation is not accomplished by satisfying an offended God with an atoning sacrifice.
2. The death of Jesus is not described in the Gospels as an atoning sacrifice.
3. New life in Christ is described as a gift of God's loving grace.

The Gospels describe Jesus as the Eternal Son become incarnate to save sinful people from "perishing" in the alienation of their sinfulness. Jesus is recorded to have been in the temple and synagogues, but he was teaching about holy living and made no emphasis on the widely practiced rituals and sacrifices of Jewish religion. (In fact, he tended to disregard and correct them.) Jesus gave no indication that sacramental rituals could cleanse sinners of their guilt and create for them a status of acceptance with God.

The Gospels describe the death of Jesus as resulting, on the one hand, from the machinations of Jewish leaders who would not accept his teachings about God. (They considered him a blasphemer who threatened their privileged positions because of his popularity with the common people.) And, on the other hand, the death of Jesus resulted from the spineless caving of the Roman governor to the blackmail threats of those scheming Jewish leaders.

Jesus is recorded (Mark 10:45, Matthew 20:28) to have said, "For the Son of Man also came not to be served but to serve, and to give his life as a ransom for many." This, however, does not necessarily mean that he was referring to his crucifixion as an "atoning blood sacrifice," for the whole meaning of incarnation is so much larger than the single event of his crucifixion. Paul expressed an inspired truth in his letter to the Philippians. In the *kenosis* (emptying) passage in Philippians 2:5-11, he wrote about the awesomely eternal meaning of incarnation, "...though he [Jesus] was in the form of God, [he] did not count equality with God a thing to be grasped [my translation: "a station to be clung to"], but emptied himself, taking the form of a servant, being born in the likeness of men."

I am persuaded that when Jesus spoke of "giving his life," he was referring to the totality of the incarnation by which he made personal revelation of the character of God, the loving care of God, and the yearning desire of God to have sinful people reconciled to transformed faith in and fellowship with himself. Everything about the life and ministry of Jesus reflects the loving initiative of God to win the trust of and reconcile unto himself the wandering "people of his pasture, and the sheep of his hand" (Psalms 95:7).

What did Jesus say about how the lost could be saved? The most significant words on this subject are found in the Gospel records about the way Jesus described the good news of God: "The kingdom of God is at hand; Repent, and believe in the gospel" (Mark 1:14-15). The words "repent" and "gospel" are central.

Repent is a powerful word that means so much more than that you are sorry that you have erred. The New Testament word is *metanoeite*. It is a plural imperative (something for everybody to do) of a verb that meant to change your mind, to change the way you think and feel about something, to change the principles and practices of your life. The context in which Jesus used the word leads me to believe that he made an imperative call for people to change their minds about how they think about God, about the priorities they pursue in their lives, about what they believe to be important enough to invest their lives in, and the practices they follow as a result of those changes. Repentance means that the arrogant rebellion of our Garden of Eden experience is changed when our knee shall bow and our tongue confess that Jesus Christ is Lord (Philippians 2:9-10). This is a real change in mind, in values, in what you trust, and in life.

The Christian religious vocabulary includes the graphic word "conversion"—to become something different than what you were before. This kind of dynamic change and reordering of life is reflected in what Jesus said to Nicodemus about being "born again (born from above)." Paul wrote, "If anyone be 'in Christ' he is a new creation."

To follow up on his call to repentance, Jesus also said, "Believe in the gospel." We would have been helped if the translators had used a clearer meaning for *euaggelion*. Its meaning is simply "good news." The good news to which Jesus was referring was the wonderful truth that the "kingdom of God is at hand"—that Jesus was in fact God present to reveal the character of God more perfectly and to make the transforming power of trusting faith and forgiving grace real to human persons.

These remembered and recorded words of Jesus were central to his preaching and reflect that repentance and faith are interrelated and interdependent as parts of our personal response to God. To believe in the gospel involves a necessary change of mind and direction of life. There is a radical difference between how unrepentant people think about God and live their lives and the values that express themselves in the life of a person who "believes the gospel." Paul described the difference in Galatians 5:19-24. Think about the difference between a life motivated by envy, jealousy, strife, anger and selfishness, and a life filled with love, joy, patience, kindness and self-control. Faith in God and the transforming help of the Holy Spirit make a "new life in Christ" difference in a person's life.

A determining difference in the way we understand our salvation experience is what role we play. Too often "getting saved" has been described as just letting God "have his way with us," that grace will bestow the gift and make our "status" forever secure in God's care. Jesus did not describe it that way. He called forth from us the hard work of life-altering repentance and a "set of the will" embracing of a new way of life lived in harmony with the very character of God himself. An experience of salvation is as much our doing as it is God's. As in so much of life, *we cannot do it without God, and God will not do it without us.* Loving grace means that God cares so much for us that the Holy Spirit is forever urging us to "repent, and believe the gospel," and grace means that God freely forgives the "walk of self-centeredness" that has kept us from a life of fellowship with him.

So salvation is a dynamically two-sided experience in which an individual and God are both involved in a reconciling event: God calls and offers, we trust his promise and respond, and God welcomes a repenting believer into his accepting fellowship. We *cannot* do it without God, and God *will not* do it without us.

I am convinced that people have been victims of an ages-long misunderstanding of God.

Among primitives, the idea of "God" was so mysterious that they thought of the supernatural as far-off and as part of their lives only in influence and requirements. The Canaanite Baals were believed to seek a place to embody themselves and a group of people they could control and use in their competition with other deities. From the time of Moses onward, the Hebrews thought of their God as dwelling "in the heavens" and ruling over them from that isolated majesty, coming into their affairs when he had directions and commands for them, to "smell the aroma of their offerings," or to chastise them for disobedience.

Even during the days of the incarnation, the Gospels reflect a concept of relationship that God the Father was "in the heavens" while Christ the Son was "walking among men." (It is no wonder that Muslims accuse Christians of not being faithful to our claim to believe in only one God.) Jesus spoke often and clearly about there being a "oneness" between Father and Son.

Our human difficulty with comprehending the relation of the physical and spiritual realms, however, has continued to mean that the theological doctrine of the omnipresence of God is largely incomprehensible to us. This "confusion of ideas" is still present in many of the images we create by the language we use. We teach children that Jesus is always with us, but then we talk to them about coming to church to "meet Jesus," as though that was where he could be found. We talk about God being everywhere, but then we begin our Sunday services with "invocations" asking God to come among us, instead of praising God (into "whose house" we have come) for inviting us to "come into his presence" and worship. I believe this lack of clarity about the "everywhere presence" of God has contributed to, and in some measure caused, a tragic neglect of the Holy Spirit.

The Tragic Neglect of the Holy Spirit

I believe neglect of the "third persona" of the Supreme God has resulted largely because of our human inability to understand the mystery of the Trinity. The word Trinity is not a biblical word, but it expresses our efforts to understand and describe the ways God's revelation of himself to humankind is set forth in the language of the Bible.

In the Old Testament, the basic portrait of God is that of creator, sovereign, and covenant God of Israel. God was believed to reside in heaven and to come into human affairs with commands for people, or to proffer blessing or judgment. This concept of the supernatural fit well into the structure of beliefs about the universe in those primitive, pre-scientific ages.

By the middle of the eighth century BC, at least one man, a prophet named Isaiah, had come to believe that God dwelt among his people. When the Syrian nation and the northern kingdom of Israel threatened the southern kingdom of Judah, King Ahaz tried to get help from Egypt. In an effort to guide King Ahaz to trust in God instead of military alliances, Isaiah told the king that a boy would soon be born and named Emmanuel, a Hebrew name meaning "God is with us" (Isaiah 7:1-16). Every day, as the boy played in the streets and his playmates called his name, "Emmanuel, Emmanuel," the words of the prophet would ring in the king's ears as a reminder, "God is with us," "God is with us." Thus God came to be known more and more as the great creator and sovereign of the world who dwelt in personal presence among his people.

When Jesus was born, God gave his presence human form to make himself known more fully and to reveal his purpose to save and to reconcile alienated sinful humanity unto himself (Matthew 1:18-25). When Matthew wrote about the birth, he declared that Jesus was indeed "God with us," not only as creator and covenant God of Israel but as Savior, as redeemer of sinful people. In the incarnation, God had taken on human personhood to make the redemptive sacrifice that could bring forgiveness and reconciliation to people who would accept Jesus for who he was and commit themselves through trusting faith to his lordship. Jesus always insisted that there was a oneness between himself and the Father, between what he was doing in incarnation and what he and the Father had been doing eternally. Father and Son are human terms used to express a concept of interrelationship within God. This does not mean they are two Gods, but that God has dimensions within his being that are beyond human capacity to comprehend.

As Jesus neared the end of his incarnate ministry and was approaching the time of his departure from a physical presence among his followers, he promised that he would not abandon them and that the Holy Spirit would come and be an abiding presence with them. I believe this promise takes on rich meaning if we understand it to be a continuation of the great truth of God's "ever-presence" since the very beginning of creation.

There is a long thread of growing human awareness of this "ever-presence" of God in the biblical records.

- The writer who compiled the book of Genesis was inspired to begin it with a story of God active in creation as a caring spirit who "hovered over the face of the waters" (Genesis 1:2) from the time the universe was still in its first "awakening."
- At the "burning bush" in the Sinai desert, God revealed himself to Moses as the great *I Am* (the uncreated, self-existing Supreme God who forever was, and from whom everything else had its existence. See Exodus 3:1-15.)
- The prophet Isaiah declared to Ahaz that the God of Israel was Emmanuel (God present with them in the times of crisis. See Isaiah 7:1-16.)
- When Matthew was inspired to record the Gospel and the revealed name Jesus (Matthew 1:18-21), he was moved to declare that this was Emmanuel (God with us to save us from our sins by forgiveness and reconciliation—verses 22-25).
- Jesus promised "another Paraclete of the same kind" (God ever-present with his people as carer, comforter, advocate, guide and help. See pages 63-65 for a fuller discussion of these ideas).

A stream of inspired understanding goes like this: God was eternal sovereign in creation; God was the great *I Am* of Hebrew faith; God was Eternal Son and incarnate Savior; and God *is* abiding presence as Eternal Holy Spirit everywhere, always calling us to faith, leading us into ways of abundant life, and loving us with unfailing love and grace.

Much of traditional Christian thought and practice has relegated the Holy Spirit to "accompanying" status (he just comes along with God the Father and Christ the Son) instead of affirming the central role that Jesus promised the Spirit would have as the Paraclete come to be Emmanuel (God with us) when the incarnation was ended. The Holy Spirit is the Eternal God accompanying us on the journey of our lives and leading us ever upward in a fellowship of love and joy, grace and forgiveness, peace and hope.

God is more than we can ever understand. The Native American Cherokees speak of hoping for a peace that "is closer than our hands or feet, closer than our breathing." The Christian faith teaches that the Holy Spirit is our God who is just that close to us always. Christian faith and practice would be immeasurably enriched by a recognition of the active role Jesus described for the Holy Spirit as Paraclete, continuing the "God with us" presence so vital to our "I-thou" relationship with God.

[1] Cited in Reinhold Seeberg, *Textbook of the History of Doctrines* (Grand Rapids: Baker Book House, 1954), Vol. I, 122-123.

[2] Cited in Seeberg, *History of Doctrines*, Vol. I, 329.

[3] Cited in Seeberg, *History of Doctrines*, Vol. I, 333-334.

[4] Cited in Seeberg, *History of Doctrines*, Vol. I, 338, 343, 359.

[5] Williston Walker, *A History of the Christian Church* (New York: Charles Scribner's Sons, 1950), 187-188.

[6] Cited in Seeberg, *History of Doctrines*, Vol. II, 153.

[7] Cited in Seeberg, *History of Doctrines*, Vol. II, 197.

[8] Cited in Seeberg, *History of Doctrines*, Vol. II, 242.

[9] Cited in Seeberg, *History of Doctrines*, Vol. II, 309.

[10] Cited in Seeberg, *History of Doctrines*, Vol. II, 398.

[11] Cited in Seeberg, *History of Doctrines*, Vol. II, 432.

[12] Cited in Seeberg, *History of Doctrines*, Vol. II, 243-244.

[13] Cited in Seeberg, *History of Doctrines*, Vol. II, 398.

[14] Edgar Young Mullins, *The Christian Religion in Its Doctrinal Expression*, (Philadelphia: The Judson Press, 1952), 294.

[15] E. Y. Mullins, *Axioms of Religion* (Nashville: Broadman & Holman Publishers, 1997), 64.

[16] Eugene H. Peterson, *The Message*, The Bible in Contemporary Language, (Colorado Springs: NavPress, 2005), Paraphrase of James 1:14.

A Presumptuous Criticism of Traditional Christianity

My personal search for revelation includes experience as a devout practicing Christian for more than 70 years, my privilege of study with some humble but learned scholars, and now a decade spent trying to understand the ways religious thought and practice have evolved through the millennia of human history. My pilgrimage has led me to the hesitant but compelling conviction that traditional Christianity has developed along two lines of belief and practice that differ from and violate the revelation Jesus made by his incarnate life and teaching. I describe the following positions as "presumptuous" and expect them to be rejected as unorthodox by many, but I must set them forth because of my heartfelt conviction that they are true.

The Role of Ritual Sacrifices

Long before the beginning of the "revealed" and later monotheistic religion of the Hebrews, the ancient animistic and nature-centered religions of primitive human tribes had developed the belief that ritual sacrifices could influence the "deities" they believed in (and most of the time simply feared). To gain favor and avoid disfavor of their deities, ancient peoples developed many elaborate ritual sacrifices.

Another aside needs to be entered here. There has developed through the eons of religious thought and practice the very human idea and attitude that the purpose of religion is to influence the supernatural (and whatever God/gods there are) for the benefit of the human practitioners of religion. Primitive peoples primarily feared the supernatural that they could not understand or control. The rituals we are discussing arose primarily for the purpose of mollifying or seeking favor and benefit from a deity.

The concept of a personal God who cares about the well-being of his people was a long time in coming into widespread belief among the Hebrews. And that belief did not reach full bloom until Jesus of Nazareth more fully revealed that God in truth is Heavenly Father, the only true God who in fundamental character is *agape* (unselfish, unfailing, eternal, outgoing, loving care for each and every human person).

There is a widely held contemporary belief that God is a justice-demanding deity so deep-seated in his offense at human sin that he will not countenance forgiveness and reconciliation without a bloody atoning sacrifice. This characterization is contrary to what Jesus revealed about the nature and character of God and his forgiving search to reconcile the world unto himself. Humble, grateful and devoted followers of Jesus Christ need to rethink the meaning and role of rituals and sacrifices against the backdrop of *agape*.

Belief in the effectiveness of ritual sacrifices to influence God/gods continued to be an integral part of Hebrew religion as it developed through the centuries. The Hebrew Scriptures of the Christian Old Testament give ample indication of how central the practice of burnt sacrifices and offerings was to the development of Judaism up to the time when Jesus lived.

The disciples of Jesus, who were the first Christians, were steeped in the faith and practice of ritual sacrifices. During Christianity's first generation, Christians were driven out of the Jewish religious institutions. The Christians began to organize into local churches for support, fellowship and worship, and within that first generation the Christian movement became primarily a Gentile religion. During that generation the Christians began to develop new rituals to replace those of Judaism that they no longer practiced.

Let us take note at this point of the role that rituals had played in the long evolutionary development of religious thought and practice. From the very first, ideas of the supernatural were about non-material forces, above and beyond material things, which influenced and controlled the material world. Those ideas developed into beliefs that gods inhabited heavenly bodies, natural objects, and some animals and people.

Since people have bodies, they have always had difficulty thinking about disembodied spirits. Religious thought has always focused on ways spiritual beings have chosen to embody themselves by inhabiting material objects. Consequently, much of religious practice through the ages has taken the form of material rituals, such as burnt sacrifices and offerings and washings for cleansing. Their aim was to do physical things to influence supernatural deities.

As the Jewish rituals were abandoned, the first Christians faced the question about ritual practices in their new religion as followers of Jesus. The two ritual practices they were able to identify as relating back to Jesus were baptism and the memorial supper. These two rituals were widely practiced from the beginning of the Christian movement—baptism as the ritual for entry into the Christian fellowship, and the memorial supper as a love feast celebrating the *koinonia* fellowship of the local Christian group.

The Doctrine and Practice of Baptism

The ritual of baptism was a carryover from a Jewish practice, but its meaning changed as it became a Christian practice. In the Hebrew/Jewish religion, washing had long been practiced as a cleansing/purifying ritual. Jews practiced immersion of non-Jews who became Jewish proselytes as a Levitical purification of their Gentile uncleanness.[1] This seems to be the background of the Essene and John the Baptist practice of immersion. John the Baptist, however, gave the practice a new meaning. He declared that repentance was the basis for immersion, indicating moral change as a required basis for the ritual cleansing.

Jesus was immersed by John at the beginning of his public ministry, and he is recorded to have said it was "to fulfill all righteousness" (Matthew 3:15). I am not sure there has been any adequate understanding or explanation of the meaning and purpose of his immersion unless it was to mark and declare his transition from carpenter to minister. It is demonstrably clear that Jesus did not place significant importance on the practice of ritual baptism.

During the early time of Jesus' ministry, there was debate about whether Jesus or John was doing the most baptisms. It is recorded in the Gospel of John that Jesus left Judea and went to Galilee to damp down any sense of competition between himself and John (3:22-23, 4:1-3). The record, however, indicates that Jesus himself did not do the baptisms. Records about the ongoing ministry of Jesus indicate declining focus on baptism; the recorded references to baptism were about John's baptism, not baptism practices by Jesus and his disciples. The references that do exist do not define clear meanings of the purpose of baptism, but the contexts recorded indicate that baptism was being practiced as an indication of repentant moral change and the beginning of a new pattern for living as a Jew or as a disciple of Jesus.

During the first generation of the Christian movement, baptism became an established Christian ritual practice. There are numerous references in the New Testament that baptism was being practiced, but there are only two references that give definitive expression to the meaning and purpose of baptism. Both are in letters by Paul and are from his late writings. In Romans 6:1-4, Paul compares a Christian's baptism to the death, burial and resurrection of Jesus. The other reference is in Colossians 2:12, where Paul also uses the burial/resurrection figure to describe conversion and the beginning of a new life in Christ. I understand this to mean that immersion depicts in dramatic ritual a personal experience of conversion, that by repentant faith and acceptance of forgiving grace an old way of life has ended and a new life of trust and fellowship with Christ has begun.

This understanding of baptism is in harmony with the words of Jesus to Nicodemus that a person must be "born again" and begin a new life to become a part of the kingdom of God (John 3:1-6). A repentant change is necessary in how

> "See" the kingdom of God (in verse 3) is the Greek word idein, the root from which we get our English word "idea," as in, "Oh, now I see, now I get it."

you think about God and life and in the values by which you live your life before you can even "begin to get the idea" of what it means to live in harmony with God. Paul made the same declaration in II Corinthians 5:17: "If anyone is *in Christ*, he is a new creation, the old has passed away, behold, the new has come."

I believe, along with those who share this understanding, that these earliest references indicate that the ritual of baptism was done by immersion as a symbolic event to give dramatic witness to an experience of conversion that had happened in a person's life through repentant faith, trusting commitment, forgiving grace, and the divine gift of new life. In his Great Commission, Jesus instructed his followers to make disciples and to baptize them. I believe his order of events gives us an indication of the proper relation of conversion and baptism.

In its earliest practice as a Christian ritual, baptism was a witness to conversion—a ritual of entry into the Christian fellowship—and not a ritual agent causing salvation. As Christianity developed as a religious movement, changes in the meaning and practice of baptism occurred. By the end of the first generation, the Jewish idea of immersion as a washing for ritual cleansing became accepted among Christians as a way to cleanse the guilt of original sin. After his third missionary journey, Paul described his conversion to the Jews in Jerusalem by saying that Ananias told him to "Rise and be baptized, and wash away your sins, calling on his [Jesus'] name" (Acts 22:16). In I Peter 3:21, one of the first documents accepted widely by the churches, baptism is described as how we are saved by water, as Noah and all in the ark were saved through water.

Early in the development of Christian beliefs about the practice of rituals, the understanding of baptism changed from a dramatic and symbolic witness to an experience of life-changing conversion into a necessary ritual sacrament, itself bestowing the grace of salvation upon the person being baptized. Thus the belief arose that baptism was necessary for salvation because it was the means by which salvation could come to a person.

Belief in baptism as a grace-bestowing ritual of salvation led to other significant changes. It seems clear that in the beginning, baptism was practiced as the immersion of believing adults in witness of their conversion to be followers of Jesus as they entered the Christian fellowship. As belief developed that baptism was a necessary sacrament of salvation, concern arose about infants who were thought to be tainted and condemned by the fated curse of original sin. Infant baptism was the church's answer.

A change in the mode of baptism for both infants and adults came to pass, evolving from immersion to pouring to sprinkling. There do not seem to be clear writings in the history of the early church to explain the rationale for the change. For instance, the Eastern national churches practice immersion even of infants. Eventually, however, baptism by sprinkling became the almost universal practice in the church under the hierarchal leadership of the popes in Rome. My attempt to understand this evolution in the mode of baptism has led me to conclude that it was most likely an adaptation caused by the perceived need to baptize infants and the infirm for their salvation when immersion was not practical, especially during the harsh medieval winters in central and northern Europe.

> Eastern national churches are those that followed the leadership of the Patriarch of Constantinople in the schism between East and West in AD 1054.

Protestant denominations that practice infant baptism but do not hold a doctrine of sacramental salvation by the ritual of baptism have generally developed some modification of the meaning of baptism, such as affirmation of birth into the covenant fellowship of the Christian family.

The rise of a belief in baptism as a necessary ritual sacrament of salvation led to another vital question about who could be an authorized officiant of baptism. That concern was part of another feature of the growing Christian movement in its earliest formative generations.

The Development of a Sacramental Priesthood

A transforming systemic change in Christian practice came with the development of an endowed priesthood within Christianity. Centuries of tradition lay behind a question that faced the first generations of Christians: "Who has authority to define and control religious beliefs and practices, and what is the source of that authority?" The Palestinian Jewish Christians came out of a religious heritage in Judaism with a long tradition of inherited, anointed, established priesthood— the sons of Aaron—from the time of Moses. The first generation of Christians embraced and exalted an authoritative status for the twelve apostles because of their first-person association with Jesus before his death. Early records seem to indicate they were recognized as the first bishops. Biblical writings about the first Christian groups indicate that elders were recognized, as they had long been recognized among the Jews, as persons with authority in religion on the basis of wisdom gained by experience and age. Paul made a practice of appointing elders to places of leadership in the churches he established and guided by visits and letters (see Acts 14:23). There is no indication, however, that the role of elder involved any priestly or sacramental function.

> The office of bishop developed as the role of clerical overseer of one or more local churches.

As Christianity spread more widely in the Mediterranean Graeco-Roman world and became a more Gentile religious movement, questions arose about who was qualified to be a leader in the local church communities. The developing traditions as reflected in Matthew 16:18-19, which became a written record about the end of the first Christian generation, held that Simon Peter had been given special status by Jesus. Belief in the primacy of Peter did not become a dominant position until the time of Augustine at the end of the fourth century AD.[2] Augustine held to "the primacy of the apostolic chair," not to "the primacy of Peter." His position was that the role of bishop (overseer) belonged to all of the apostles equally, and from them the "trail of bishops followed."[3]

The development of a priestly role for Christian clergy did not come for more than two centuries. Cyprian of Carthage (about AD 250) is reported to be the first of the church fathers "to assert an actual priesthood of the clergy, based on the sacrifice offered by them."[4]

> The sacrifice referred to was the Lord's Supper, which from about AD 150, along with baptism, had come to be believed in as rituals necessary for salvation and eternal life.

Belief in baptism and the Lord's Supper as salvation-bestowing sacramental rituals and belief in a priestly role for clergy were inter-related developments in early Christianity. After all, if baptism and the Lord's Supper bestow salvation and eternal life, who is endowed, and by whom, with ability and authority to perform these rituals? Thus the question about clergy ordination was a part of the early Christian movement.

The first step in the development process was acceptance that Jesus so endowed the twelve apostles, and they became the first recognized bishops (overseers) of local churches. More than twelve bishops were needed for the growing number of churches. The next step was that the churches accepted the idea that these apostle bishops, commissioned by Jesus, were granted by God to have the authority to identify and endow by anointing through ordination other bishops as they were needed by the churches.

By the last half of the second century, the widespread belief developed within Christianity that the bishop overseers were the established channels of truth and doctrine for the churches. By that time it had become accepted that the bishop was in complete control of the life of the church, and while the office of bishop was highly esteemed, the authority of an individual bishop was still limited to the local church where he held office. The bishop's control over the life of the church was supremely manifested in his control of the rituals of baptism and the Lord's Supper. Only the bishop could administer these grace-bestowing sacraments.

Since bishops were finite men, incidents occurred where some failed to measure up to the high moral and spiritual standards incumbent upon the office. Questions arose and were sharply debated about whether ordination bestowed an "indelible character" on a person so that his administration of sacraments was effective. Some of the church fathers insisted "yes," and others insisted "no."

In a major controversy at the beginning of the fourth century AD, a group called Donatists held that the administrator must be "valid" for the ritual to be "valid"—that is, the priest must be a faithful holy man for his administration of ritual sacraments to be effective. Augustine and the catholic fathers held that God worked through the ritual and made grace effective even if the administering clergy was a heretic or immoral person. At the Council of Arles in AD 316, Augustine and his group prevailed.[5] It became established doctrine in the stream of Christianity that developed into the Roman Catholic Church that the sacraments of baptism and ordination made transforming changes in the very nature of the person baptized or ordained. A proper officiant for the rituals was important, but the sacrament was believed to be the work of God and was effective even if the performer of the ritual was unworthy. The inherent sacramental change in nature is believed to be fixed, perpetual and indelible.[6] Hence the baptized cannot become lost and the ordained cannot become unanointed. Dissenters, free church Christians, and "priesthood of all believers" Christians have not embraced those doctrines of baptism and ordination.

The developing role of priestly function for the clergy, along with anointed capacity and authority to bestow sacramental grace as central to that priestly role, became a basic feature of the rise of hierarchical control of doctrine and practice by the late sixth century AD, when Gregory I as Bishop of Rome was able to effectively consolidate papal dominance over the Roman Catholic Church.

It seems to me that the rise of belief in rituals as channels for bestowal of grace, and the rise of belief in a priestly role for clergy, are a developed departure in traditional Christianity from the revelation made by Jesus about the way God relates to individual persons and to the community of those who seek to follow and serve him.

There have arisen through the millennia many kinds of religious leaders, proclaimers of religious ideas, and practitioners of religious rituals. The history of behavior by religious leaders indicates that too many were men of arrogant ambition who used claims of influence with the supernatural to manipulate individuals and groups for their personal benefit, influence and status. It is also true that many more religious leaders used any capacity they had in altruistic ways to serve the needs of others. So the history of religious leaders reflects that some were good and some were bad, depending upon the character, integrity and motivation of men (and women) who have practiced religious leadership.

In the Hebrew and Christian faiths in particular, there has been present throughout their 4,000-year history a well-established heritage of belief that persons have been "called out and endowed" by God. I have no doubt whatever about the activity of God's Holy Spirit in stirring the inner soul of individuals to be keenly aware of endowed abilities and the challenge of opportunity to serve human need and high purpose. But the idea that Jewish priests and Christian clergy have any transformed nature, infallible insight and supernatural anointing simply will not hold water in light of the clear record of these millennia of history.

As a person who has spent my adult lifetime in religious leadership and moved in collegial association with Christian clergy, I am painfully aware that humans are fallible. There have been untold millions who have served with holy motivation and have sought little except a humble opportunity to represent God faithfully and serve people effectively and unselfishly. But there have been enough (far more than there should have been) who have "worn the mantle" but have done so with arrogant ambition and selfish purpose.

After more than six decades as an "ordained Christian minister," I am deeply convinced that religious leadership is a role favored by God, guided by God (if the person involved is willing to be so led), and used by God to extend his loving grace to the human race. I am convinced, however, that this role is to be open to the leading of the Holy Spirit, to be a bearer of the good news of the light of truth about God and from God, to be a living example of the high standards of right and good that reflect the holy character of God, and to encourage others to embrace an experience of life-changing repentance through trusting faith, which leads to genuine reconciliation with God. The true role of a minister does not involve ritual bestowal of benefit by one person upon another, for nothing done outside a person can change the nature and character of that person. Authentic salvation is something that happens inside a person through faith in the loving forgiveness and accepting grace of God, which truly transform a person and bring new life.

This also means that rituals do not have any sacramental power to bestow grace upon a person. Rituals can be powerful experiences, but their meaning and power must come from what a person puts into them, not from any bestowal that comes from them.

I come to this conviction from what I believe to be revealed insight that came to the ancient Hebrew prophet Micah. We are not made right with and brought into harmony with God by "sacrificing rams on altars and offering rivers of oil." People have proven convincingly that they can walk up to altars and perform rituals and walk away the same as they were before. What counts with God is when we love justice, do kindness, and live by trust in him. (See Micah 6:6-8.) Jesus was very clear about it. He said, "You must be born again," and he did not spell out any rituals by which it happens. His words were, "Repent and believe the gospel." I can only conclude that traditional Christianity has gone astray when it has changed or added to Jesus' words.

Toward A Recovery of True Sacrament

Now some words about sacraments. I find no evidence from Jesus to indicate that there are any physical rituals that humans can perform that convey the grace of salvation or special status with God. But I do believe in sacraments and wish that Christians could believe and experience them. I believe any experience in which somehow God's spirit touches a human spirit and makes that moment a sacred moment is indeed a sacrament of grace. It can happen at a person's baptism, in an observance of the Lord's Supper, when you see a sunrise, when you hold a newborn baby, when you read and meditate on a passage of Scripture, or any time or place when your heart and soul are open and responsive to God. But I am convinced that sacraments happen when you and God meet in a sacred experience, not when some person performs a ritual involving you. All of this simply means that I am a practicing, free church, "priesthood of all believers" kind of Christian who dares to study the history of religion and "think outside the box" of traditional Christian interpretations and practices. I may be wrong, but I am willing to meet my Lord with my devotion to him, trusting in his forgiving grace, and believing he will grant me an eternity of "becoming" more like him.

---

[1] Sherman E. Johnson, "Exegesis of Matthew," *The Interpreter's Bible*, 7 (1951): 264.
[2] Reinhold Seeberg, *Textbook of the History of Doctrines* (Grand Rapids: Baker Book House, 1954), Vol. I, 180.
[3] Seeberg, *History of Doctrines*, Vol. I, 318.
[4] Seeberg, *History of Doctrines*, Vol. I, 182.
[5] Seeberg, *History of Doctrines*, Vol. I, 314, 319.
[6] Seeberg, *History of Doctrines*, Vol. I, 319-320.

Summary and Conclusion

There is clear and undeniable evidence that there has been incremental evolutionary growth and development in human knowledge. Bit by bit through the ages, people have learned more and more about natural law, universal cosmology, human biology, physics, etc. It was many centuries before any humans began to understand gravity, tides, seasons, the sun-centered cosmos, and even something as common to primitives as animal and human reproduction. It was even longer before people discovered electricity, bacteria, viruses, atoms, penicillin, and now digital technology.

It is equally evident and undeniable that through the last 25,000 years there has been significant evolutionary development and change in the meaning of religious thought and the formulation of religious practices. It took a long time for people to develop belief in the supernatural as an answer to their questions about the natural world. Many more years passed before people began to formulate concepts about the relationship of the natural physical world and the non-material spiritual world.

Eventually, human searching (and I believe divine guidance) brought the human race to fashion a concept of supernatural spiritual beings that controlled physical events in nature and in human life. The idea of "the divine" came into being, and people began to think of deities (gods) who were supernatural and affected their lives in many ways. So humans began to try to influence those deities for their personal and tribal benefit. Their basic questions were, "How can I make the god who is 'watching' me happy?" and "How can I keep from making that god unhappy?" Religion and religious practices were born.

This was not merely human activity and achievement. As a theistic evolutionist, I am convinced that every step and stage in the process of physical and spiritual development was designed, enabled and guided by the Supreme Eternal God who in the fullness of time revealed himself as the Heavenly Father of our Lord Jesus Christ. All the ages involved were God's way of raising up a species of human persons who have the capacity for rational thought, freedom and ability to make choices and live them out, and moral and spiritual sensitivity to perceive worth and consequence in human action. God chose, for reasons only he could disclose but has not, to create a species of beings called the human race who could relate to him in an I-thou, Person-to-person relationship. Insofar as we know, everything else in existence has an I-it, Person-to-thing relationship to God, controlled by him through natural law or evolved instinct.

When the capacity for religious sensitivity developed in the human race, religious thought and practice began. I believe God has always been actively involved, helping enlightenment and understanding develop incrementally. The process has been ages long, but the search and growth had to be human, and the experience had to be human if we were to be in a true I-thou relationship in which each person (God and a human individual) is involved by free choice and with trust in the other party.

To the most ancient primitives, the unexplainable mystery of the influence of heavenly bodies like the sun and moon and the very present power and influence of natural objects like wind, rain, rivers and tides caused people to identify such objects as things to worship, worship being for them largely awe-inspired fear. As an awareness of spiritual reality developed, belief arose that spiritual beings (deities or demons) inhabited those natural objects and controlled people's lives through them. Rituals of burnt sacrifices developed as practices the people believed would please the gods and gain favor and reward from them, or assuage the disfavor of the gods and bring exemption or respite from their anger.

Such beliefs about the nature and character of the supernatural gave rise to the origins of religious thought and the development of religious practices that prevailed in the nature and animistic religions in the first primitive centuries of religious consciousness. As human knowledge grew incrementally and society advanced, the "hunting, gathering" way of life became more "herding, tribal" in nature. Religious thought also developed and advanced. The supernatural came to be thought of less as impersonal power and more as personal spirit. "The Supernatural," as in the many nature gods of primitive polytheism, gave way to belief in "The Supreme God" in the developed monotheism of late Judaism, Christianity and Islam.

These three great monotheistic religions all have affirmed from their beginning a base in revelation. Abraham said, "God called me to go." The Hebrew prophets claimed that God told them to speak to the people. Muhammad said an angel appeared to him in visions and revealed to him the text of the Golden Koran in heaven, and he was able to memorize it word for word and produce the Koran used in Islam on earth. And the Christian faith claims the highest revelation in the self-revelation of God in the incarnate person of Jesus of Nazareth.

The records of all those revelations are deemed sacred writings in the Hebrew Scriptures of the Old Testament, in the New Testament canon of the Christian Bible, and in the Koran of Islam. To multitudes in each of the religions, these writings are held to be so sacred that they are inerrant and infallible, and it is heretical to even think of questioning them. The truth, however, is that none of these writings speak with a single voice. The documents themselves have been modified through the centuries both by editors and by interpreters. And while they have been abused, misused and desecrated by some, they have been esteemed, treasured and trusted for guidance by multitudinous millions through the centuries.

These sacred documents do describe differing facets of the nature and character of the God they declare to reveal. The most prominent feature of God set forth in both the Hebrew Scriptures and the Koran is that of a reigning king who requires loyalty and obedience from his subjects and demands the justice of chastisement for disobedience. God is described as both kind and vengeful. So it depends on which portion of their sacred writings a Jew or Muslim chooses to follow that causes them to be peaceful or violent in their application of their religion. One of the most obvious differences between the two religious groups is that Hebrews claim they are God's chosen people through the Isaac line of descendants from Abraham, while the Muslims claim they are God's chosen people through the Ishmael and Esau line of descendants from Abraham.

The Christian faith makes a different claim, based on the life and teachings of Jesus of Nazareth.

This brings me to an attempt to summarize what I believe as the core of my religious convictions and the heart of my religious commitment. It is based upon my study of the historic origins and development of religious thought and practice, upon my personal religious experience of more than seventy years, and primarily upon my understanding of the incarnation of the Eternal Son of God in the person of Jesus of Nazareth.

As I have stated earlier, I am a Jesus theologian because I am convinced that through Jesus God did a unique thing—a self-revelation that put a new face on God and on the meaning of religion. We understand so little about God, for infinity is more than finite minds can even begin to comprehend. I believe this is the reason there have been so many varied concepts of the supernatural in the eons of human development and in humanity's search for insight and truth about reality.

The life and teachings of Jesus, however, demonstrate and reflect wonderfully awesome truths about the nature, character and purposes of God. The influence of their exposure to his life and teachings was enough to convince a small band of followers to believe that he was indeed the Eternal Son of God become incarnate as a human person. His transforming influence on their lives was enough to make them a band of trusting and faithful believers who became the beginning nucleus of the worldwide Christian movement.

Jesus helped his followers understand the truth that "God is love." The most fundamental nature of God is *agape*, usually translated "love." But it means so much more than the meaning put into the word and concept of "love" in contemporary western culture.[1] *Agape* means that the character of a person is outreaching in care for others, unselfish in attitude toward others, compassionate in concern for others, desirous to bestow blessings on others, unwilling to hold a grudge against another, unwilling to let offenses be a barrier to fellowship with another, and motivated to actively seek reconciliation with any alienated person. This a picture of a *big* God, a true God of love. Jesus revealed that the Supreme God, his Father, our Heavenly Father, is such a God, and God has established at the heart of the universe he created a moral law that the most fundamental good human persons can do for one another is to relate to them in *agape*.

Jesus also helped his followers to understand that God is a giving God. Jesus said of himself that he had not come into the world to be served but to serve, and to give his life as a ransom for many. (See Mark 10:45, and my discussion of this passage on page 102.) Jesus was very clear that God, in his dealing with humanity, was not about what he, God, could get out of it for himself. God has always been motivated by his *agape* (care) for us to be active in seeking what he can give to us and how he can bless us. This is a very different picture of the character of God that was and is often portrayed in pre-Christian beliefs and in some doctrines set forth in some systems of theology among Christians. Jesus did not talk about any "imperial privileges" of God deriving from his divine sovereignty, nor did he talk about God doing anything for his self-enhancement. All of his focus was on God's concern about what he could do for us.

But someone will say that this does not take sinfulness seriously. God cannot simply ignore the arrogant rebellion that alienates humans from God. I answer, "Not at all." Remember that in the parable of the Garden of Eden, Adam and Eve did not have to leave the garden because God was angry with them but because their rebellious, disobedient character meant they no longer belonged in the garden. God does not ignore sinfulness, but he does not angrily punish with a demand for justice. Because God loves us, he wants to redeem us—that is, he wants to bring about a transformation of our very nature so that we belong in harmonious fellowship with him. Paul's words have rich enlightened inspiration in them: ". . . in Christ God was reconciling the world unto himself, not counting their trespasses against them" (II Corinthians 5:19).

In his preaching, Jesus set forth how this reconciliation takes place. Mark recorded that the basic message of Jesus' preaching was, "The kingdom of God is at hand, repent, and believe in the gospel" (1:15; see my discussion of this passage on page 102-104).

If our rebellious choices and the values by which we live cause us to be "out of sync" with God, then we do not belong in the edenic garden of his fellowship. Only by repenting, only by a transforming change in the way we think about God, in the choices we make and the values we live by, only by believing in the gospel, only by a repentant trusting in the forgiving grace of God, and only by the transforming conversion of a "new birth from above" can our reconciliation with God become a reality. God takes sinfulness very seriously, and until we do there is no hope for us.

But Jesus did not indicate by his teaching or by the practices he followed that this transforming change takes place through rituals or sacraments performed by us or others. Jesus gave every indication that it is by our freedom of choice and our actions of will, as "spirit-persons" created in the image of God, who is the supreme eternal SPIRIT-PERSON, that we respond in repentant and trusting faith to his loving grace, leave our prodigal self-centeredness, and come home "to our Father's house."

Then, again, I hear someone say, "But it is all God's grace." Well, "yes" and "no." That treasured biblical word is, "We are saved by grace through faith," and yes, it does say this is not our own doing but is a gift of God. But faith is *our* faith or it is not ours at all, and you can be sure of this: "We cannot do it without God, and God will not do it without us." The gracious Holy Spirit of God is always seeking to lead us to repentant faith and acceptance of God's loving forgiveness and redeeming grace. That is how our "out of sync" sinfulness becomes "reconciled harmony" and new life in Christ.

And indeed, it is all of grace. Be sure of this: You can never move first in your relationship with God. God has always already moved in initiatives of love and grace to reveal himself, to offer forgiveness, to seek reconciliation. He established the I/thou, Person-to-person relationship as he raised up human persons capable of "having-to-do" personally with him. It is all of grace and not deserved by us. If he had not made us to be the kind of beings we are, there would never have been any possibility of a relationship with him, and if he had abandoned us and cast us off in our sinfulness, we would indeed have perished.

So I conclude that God caused us to be because he wanted to have a personal relationship with us in which he could give the blessings of his love and care and providence, and in which we would be able as persons to respond by free choice to love him in return, to trust him for the gift of abundant eternal life, and to live forever with him in this world and the next in a fellowship of ever-expanding goodness and glory.

In the divine mystery that was the incarnation of the Eternal Son of God in the human person of Jesus of Nazareth, God made a self-revelation of wonderful truths about himself, about his character, about the dynamic of his *agape* love, and about his gracious readiness and desire to forgive, redeem and reconcile us from our prodigal wandering into a fellowship of harmony that Jesus called "abundant life." Religious thought had not reached that divine level before Jesus lived. We cannot reach higher. Our highest callings and richest hopes are to embrace the God whom Jesus revealed and to make our lives, with the help of the Holy Spirit, a practice of trusting faith and obedience.

---

[1]G. Abbott-Smith, A Manual Greek Lexicon of the New Testament (Edinburgh: T. & T. Clark, 1950), 3-4. See also William F. Arndt & F. Wilbur Gingrich, A Greek-English Lexicon of the New Testament (Chicago: University of Chicago Press, 1979), 5-6.

www.ingramcontent.com/pod-product-compliance
Lightning Source LLC
Chambersburg PA
CBHW070938180426
43192CB00039B/2336